This book is dedicated to all students of the Red School House — past, present and future.

ISBN 1-893487-00-8

To all who read this material: The author has been careful not to profane any of the Ojibway teachings. He has attempted to leave the sacred teachings intact where their complete form has been proclaimed by ritual. This book is only a glimpse into the magnitude and depth of the spiritual history and heritage of the people from whom it came...the Ojibway Anishinabe.

Note: The Mishomis Coloring Book series, covering the first five chapters of the Mishomis Book and other Ojibway language materials and tapes are now available along with many other culturally oriented products. For more information on our other products, write or call us at the address and telephone number given below.

Published and distributed by:
Indian Country Communications Inc.
7831N Grindstone Ave.
Hayward, Wisconsin 54843-2052
(715) 634-5226

Printed in the United States of America

ACKNOWLEDGEMENTS

Mishomis is the Ojibway word for grandfather. **The Mishomis Book** comes from the words passed down by grandfathers and grandmothers. The author wishes to recognize the contribution of his elders from the Lac Courte Oreilles Reservation and other Indian communities in Wisconsin. Mi-gwetch forever to the following:

Grandfather: William Hart — Naw-shoo-gwun′ (eighth degree Mide priest)
Mother: Nancy Hart Benton — Ah-ni-koo′-gaw-bow-we-qway′ (third degree Mide woman)
Father: Joseph Benton — Zhing-goo-gee′-shig ah-ki-wen-see′
Stepfather: John Barber — O-za-wi′-be-nay′
Namesake: John Mink — Zhoo-ni-ya-gee′-shig
Elders: John Stone — Ba-skway′-gin
Jim Pipe Mustache — O-pwa′-gun
William Webster
Archie Mosay

There are countless others that should be recognized: men, women, elders, scroll teachers, participants and believers of the Original Way, the Midewiwin.

This book is the result of many periods of fasting, meditation, consultation, dreaming, and listening to the quiet voice of the Creator who speaks not to the ear but to the soul. Perhaps the highest and most important influence in the development of this material was prayer and belief in the Sacred Way of the Midewiwin.

Editor and illustrator: Joe Liles

helpful advice from: Walter (Porky) White
Cherie Neima
Naomi Lyons

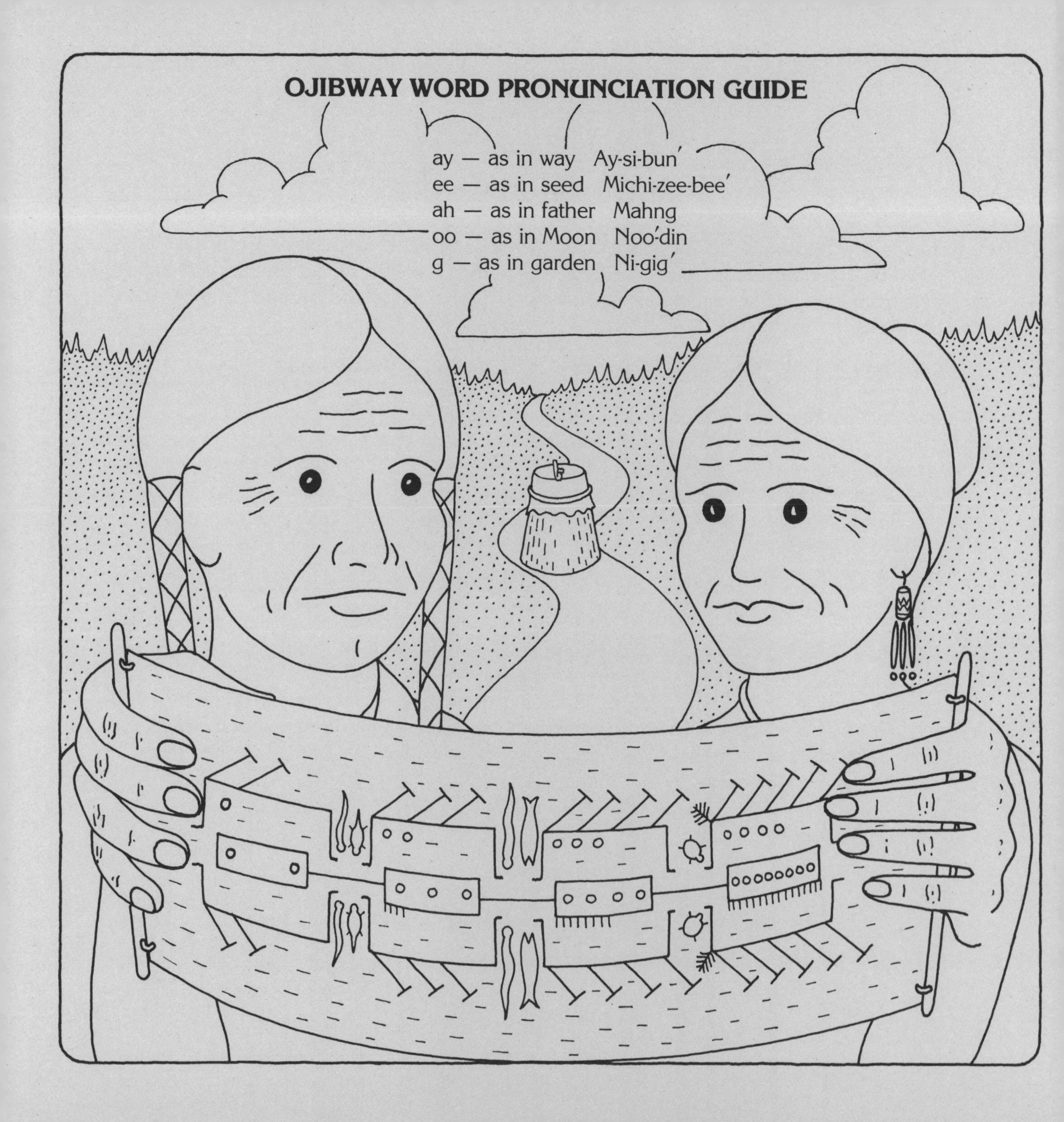
OJIBWAY WORD PRONUNCIATION GUIDE
ay — as in way Ay-si-bun′
ee — as in seed Michi-zee-bee′
ah — as in father Mahng
oo — as in Moon Noo′din
g — as in garden Ni-gig′

Mishomis in his cabin

Chapter 1

The Ojibway Creation Story

Boo-zhoo' (hello), my name is Mishomis. I am an Ojibway Indian. I live here in my cabin on the forested shores of Madeline Island. Madeline Island is in Lake Superior and is part of a group of islands now called the Apostle Islands. It is not far from the city of Ashland, Wisconsin. Many years ago, my Ojibway ancestors migrated to this area from their original homeland on the eastern shores of North America. Now the Ojibways and their offshoots are spread from the Atlantic coast, all along the St. Lawrence River, and throughout the Great Lakes region of this country. Madeline Island was the final stopping place on this great migration. Here, the Waterdrum of the traditional Midewiwin Lodge sounded its voice loud and clear. Its voice traveled far over the water and through the woodlands. Its voice attracted the many bands of the Ojibway until this island became the capital of the Ojibway nation.

It has been many years since the Waterdrum has sounded its voice here. This Waterdrum that I have beside me was handed down from my grandfathers. I am preparing this place to be a place of rebirth for traditional Indian ways. I am

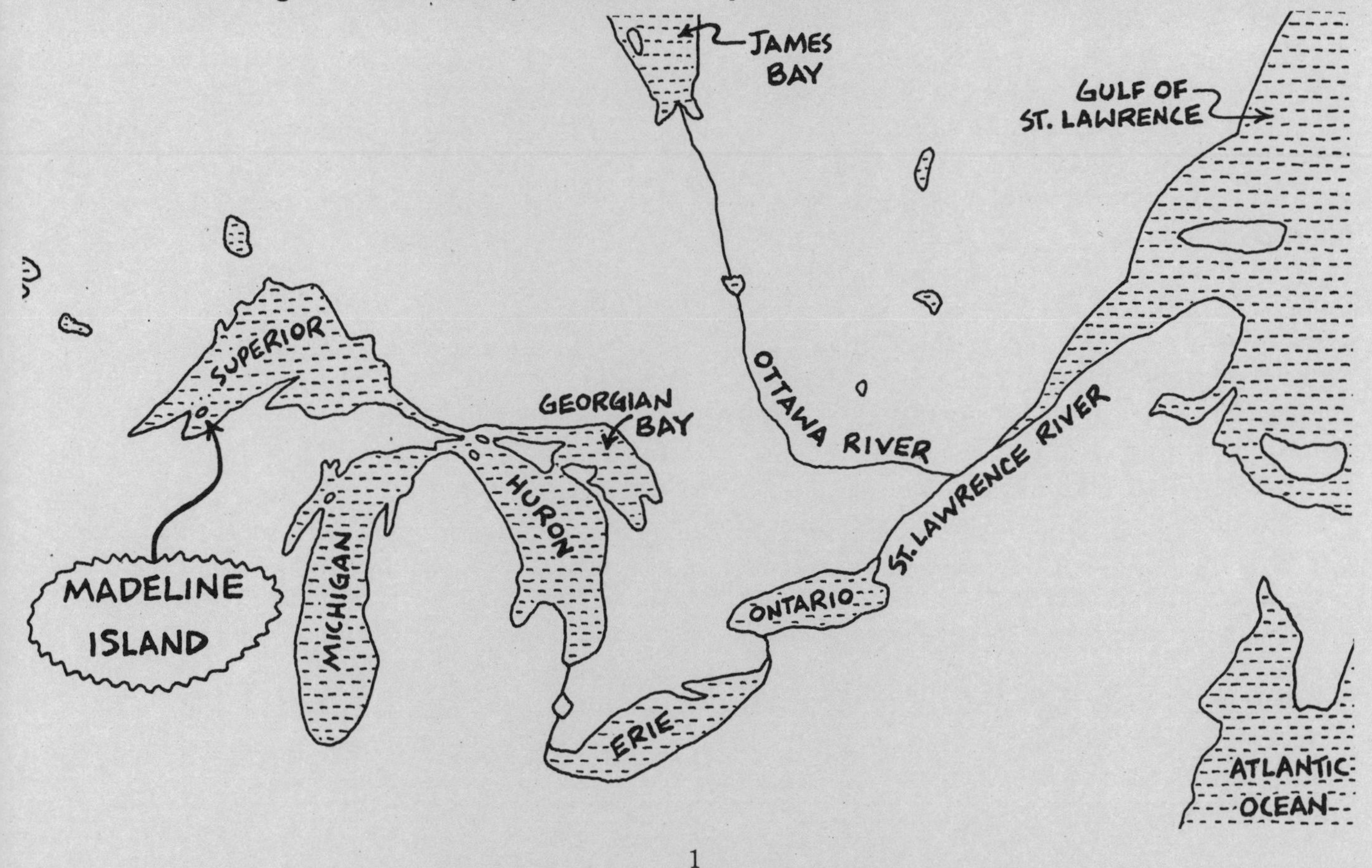

preparing myself so that I might remember the teachings of my grandfathers. I would like to give these teachings to you. I believe that, together, we can begin the journey back to find what many of our people left by the trail. This will be a journey to rediscover a way of life that is centered on the respect for all living things. It will be a journey to find the center of ourselves so that we can know the peace that comes from living in harmony with powers of the Universe. I do not believe in isolating myself in the memories of the past. I do believe that with the teachings of yesterday we can better prepare ourselves for the uncertainties of tomorrow.

I hope you will take these words that I seek to put down and use them in a good way. Use them to teach your children about the way life has developed for the Native people of this country. Use them to redirect your life to the principles of living in harmony with natural world.

I would like to tell you an account of how man was created on this Earth. This teaching was handed down by word of mouth from generation to generation by my ancestors. Sometimes the details of teachings like this were recorded on scrolls made from Wee'-gwas (birchbark). I am fortunate to be the keeper of several of these scrolls. They will help me remember some of the details of what I give to you.

When Ah-ki' (the Earth) was young, it was said that the Earth had a family. Nee-ba-gee'-sis (the Moon) is called Grandmother, and Gee'-sis (the Sun) is called Grandfather. The Creator of this family is called Gi'-tchie Man-i-to' (Great Mystery or Creator).

The Earth is said to be a woman. In this way it is understood that woman preceded man on the Earth. She is called Mother Earth because from

her come all living things. Water is her life blood. It flows through her, nourishes her, and purifies her.

On the surface of the Earth, all is given Four Sacred Directions—North, South, East, and West. Each of these directions contributes a vital part to the wholeness of the Earth. Each has physical powers as well as spiritual powers, as do all things.

When she was young, the Earth was filled with beauty.

The Creator sent his singers in the form of birds to the Earth to carry the seeds of life to all of the Four Directions. In this way life was spread across the Earth. On the Earth the Creator placed the swimming creatures of the water. He gave life to all the plant and insect world. He placed the crawling things and the four-leggeds on the land. All of these parts of life lived in harmony with each other.

Gitchie Manito then took four parts of Mother Earth and blew into them using a Sacred Shell.

From the union of the Four Sacred Elements and his breath, man was created.

It is said the Gitchie Manito then lowered man to the Earth. Thus, man was the last form of life to be placed on the Earth. From this Original Man came the A-nish-i-na'-be people.

In the Ojibway language if you break down the word Anishinabe, this is what it means:

ANI	NISHINA	ABE
FROM WHENCE	LOWERED	THE MALE OF THE SPECIES

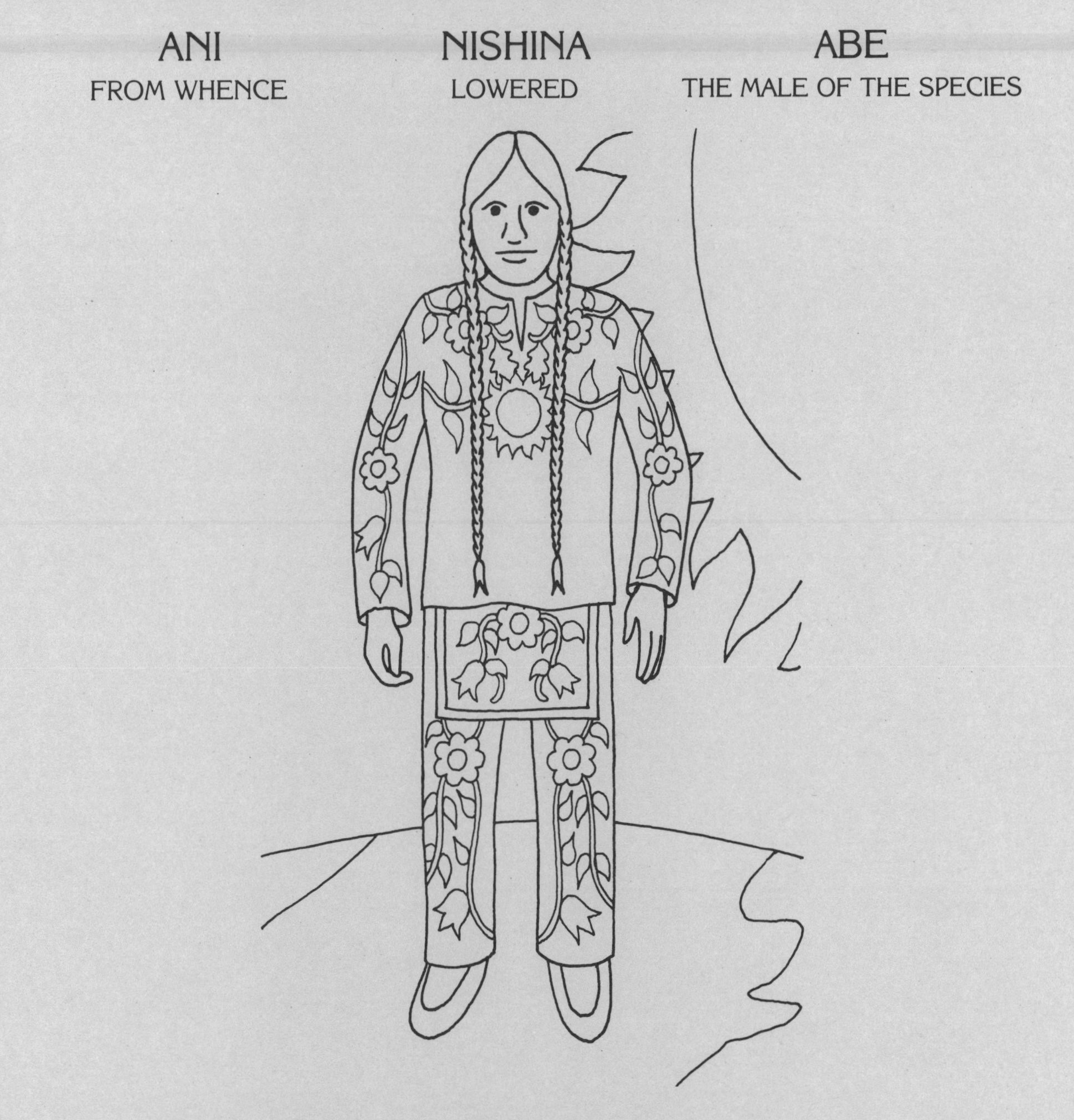

This man was created in the image of Gitchie Manito. He was natural man. He was part of Mother Earth. He lived in brotherhood with all that was around him.

All tribes came from this Original Man. The Ojibway are a tribe because of the way they speak. We believe that we are nee-kon′-nis-ug′ (brothers) with all tribes; we are separated only by our tongue or language.

Today, the Ojibways cherish the Megis Shell as the Sacred Shell through which the Creator blew his breath. The Megis was to appear and re-appear to the Ojibway throughout their history to show them the Path that the Creator wished them to follow. Some Ojibway Indians today wear the Megis or Cowrie shell to remember the origin of man and the history of their people.

There are a few people in each of the tribes that have survived to this day who have kept alive their teachings, language, and religious ceremonies. Although traditions may differ from tribe to tribe, there is a common thread that runs throughout them all. This common thread represents a string of lives that goes back all the way to Original Man.

Today, we need to use this kinship of all Indian people to give us the strength necessary to keep our traditions alive. No one way is better than another. I have heard my grandfathers say that there are many roads to the High Place. We need to support each other by respecting and honoring the "many roads" of all tribes. The teachings of one tribe will shed light on those of another.

It is important that we know our native language, our teachings, and our ceremonies so that we will be able to pass this sacred way of living on to our children and continue the string of lives of which we are a living part.

Mi-gwetch′ (thank-you)!

Chapter 2

Original Man Walks The Earth

Boozhoo, I have more Ojibway stories to tell you. These e-ki-na-ma'-di-win' (teachings) have been handed down to me by my Grandfathers. In the last chapter we learned of how Original Man was created and lowered to the Earth by the Creator, Gitchie Manito.

After Original Man was placed on the Earth, he was given instructions by the Creator. He was told to walk this Earth and name all the o-way-se-ug' (animals), the plants, the hills, and the valleys of the Creator's gi-ti-gan' (garden).

Original Man had no name of his own yet. Later, people would refer to him as Anishinabe and, still later, Way-na-boo'-zhoo. But at this early time, he who had no name would name all the Creation.

As Original Man walked the Earth, he named all of the ni-bi' (water). He identified all the rivers, streams, ponds, lakes and oceans. He learned that there were rivers that ran underground. These are the veins of Mother Earth. Water is her life blood. It purifies her and brings food to her.

Original Man also named all the parts of the body. He even named the o-kun-nug' (bones) and organs inside the body.

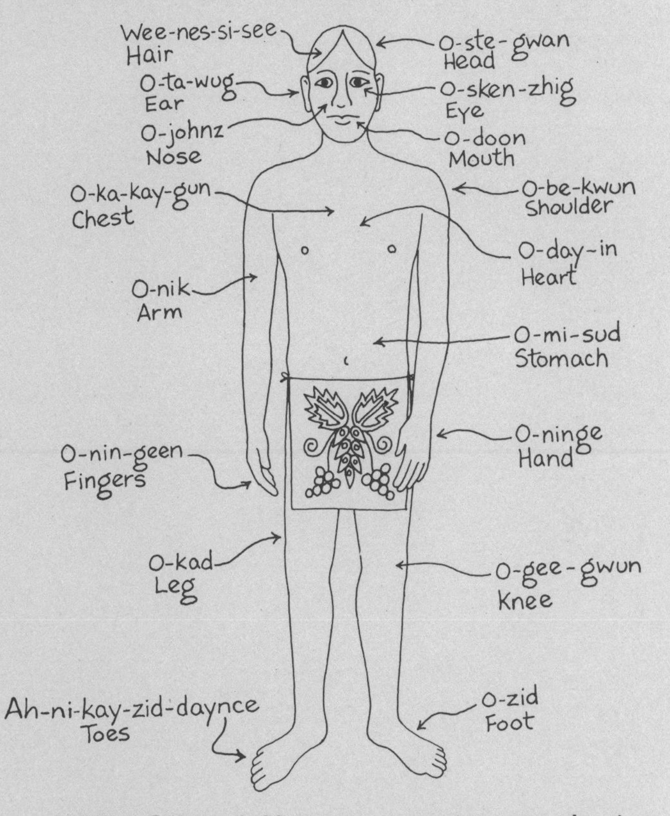

While Original Man was carrying out the instructions given to him by the Creator, he noticed that the Earth had four seasons. All life was part of a never-ending cycle.

The plants were given new life in the spring. With the coming of summer, they blossomed and bore the seeds for the next generation. Some of the plants produced fruits.

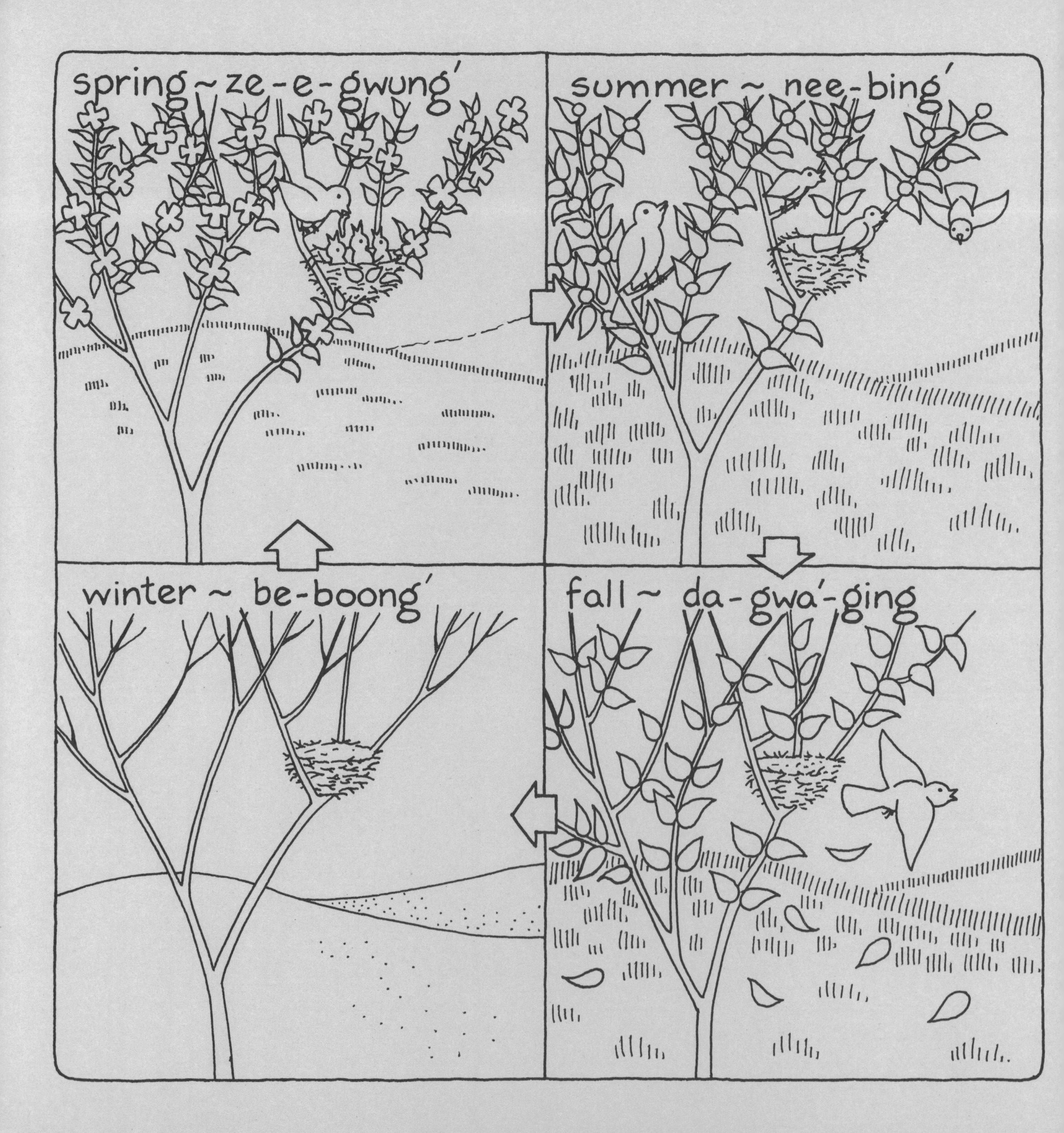
spring ~ ze-e-gwung'
summer ~ nee-bing'
winter ~ be-boong'
fall ~ da-gwa'-ging

In the fall season, the leaves of many of the plants turned from green to many spectacular colors. The leaves gradually fell to the ground as the gee-zhi-gad-doon′ (days) got shorter and the dee-bee-kad-doon′ (nights) got colder.

In winter, the cold winds of the Gee-way′-din (North) brought the purifying snows that cleansed Mother Earth. Some of the plants died and returned their bodies to their Mother. Other plants fell into a deep sleep and awoke only when Grandfather Sun and the warm winds of the Zha-wa-noong′ (South) announced the coming of spring.

As Original Man traveled the Earth, he identified what fruits were good to eat and what was not to be eaten. As he went, he found that some o-gee′-bic-coon′ (roots) were good for food. Others were good for mush-kee-ki′ (medicine). Some roots could be used to make dyes of different colors and flavorings for food. Other roots could be used as a strong thread in sewing and in making tools.

As he walked, Original Man talked with the animals. He named them as he went. He noted that some animals were good for we-sin′-ni-win′ (food) and medicine. He noticed that each type of animal had its own individual kind of wisdom. He did not know what all of these plants and animals would play an important part for all the people that would be coming to live on the Earth at a later time.

Original Man traveled everywhere. There was not one plant, animal, or place that was not touched by him.

In his travels, Original Man began to notice that all the animals came in pairs and they reproduced. And yet, he was alone.

He spoke to his Grandfather the Creator and asked, "Why am I alone? Why are there no other ones like me?"

Gitchie Manito answered, "I will send someone to walk, talk and play with you."

He sent Ma-en′-gun (the wolf).

With Ma-en'-gun by his side, Original Man again spoke to Gitchie Manito, "I have finished what you asked me to do. I have visited and named all the plants, animals, and places of this Earth. What would you now have me to do?"

Gitchie Manito answered Original Man and Ma-en'-gun, "Each of you are to be a brother to the other. Now, both of you are to walk the Earth and visit all its places."

So, Original Man and Ma-en'-gun walked the Earth and came to know all of her. In this journey they became very close to each other. They became like brothers. In their closeness they realized that they were brothers to all of the Creation.

When they had completed the task that Gitchie Manito asked them to do, they talked with the Creator once again.

The Creator said, "From this day on, you are to separate your paths. You must go your different ways.

"What shall happen to one of you will also happen to the other. Each of you will be feared, respected and misunderstood by the people that will later join you on this Earth."

And so Ma-en'-gun and Original Man set off on their different journeys.

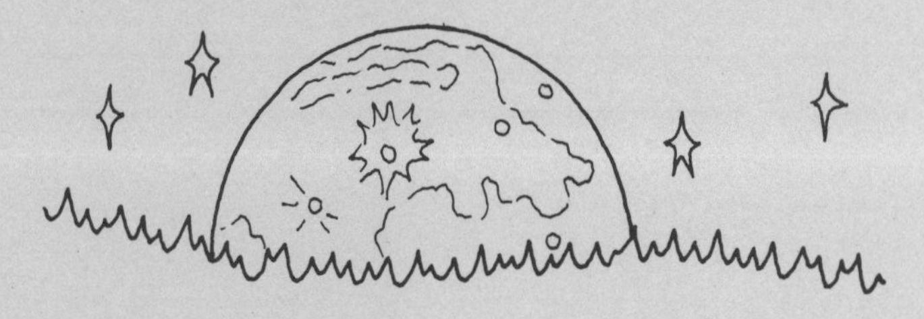

This last teaching about the wolf is important for us today. What the Grandfather said to them has come true. Both the Indian and the wolf have come to be alike and have experienced the same thing. Both of them mate for life. Both have a Clan System and a tribe. Both have had their land taken from them. Both have been hunted for their wee-nes'-si-see' (hair). And both have been pushed very close to destruction.

We can tell about our future as Indian people by looking at the wolf. It seems as though the wolf is beginning to come back to this land. Will this prove that Indian people will cease to be the "Vanishing Americans?" Will Indian people emerge to lead the way back to natural living and respect for our Earth Mother?

The teaching about wolf is important for another reason. From the wolf came the ah-ni-moosh-shug′ (dogs) that are friends to our people today. They are brothers to us much like wolf was a brother to Original Man. Because Gitchie Manito separated the paths of wolf and man, and since our dogs today are relatives of the wolf, we should never let dogs be around our sacred ceremonies. To do so would violate the Creator's wishes and endanger the lives of those participating in the ceremony. So also, dogs are not supposed to be around places where ceremonial objects are stored. Some tribes today honor dogs in special ceremonies. This is done to recognize the special brotherhood that existed between wolf and Original Man.

It is from the sacrifices that Original Man made in naming all of the Creation that our Naming Ceremonies today are taken. For this ceremony, a medicine person is asked by the father and mother of a child to seek a name for their young one. This seeking can be done through fasting, meditation, prayer, or dreaming. The Spirit World might speak to the medicine person and give a name for the young child.

At a gathering of family and friends, the medicine person burns an offering of Tobacco and pronounces the new name to each of the Four Directions. All those present repeat the name each time it is called out.

In this way the Spirit World comes to accept and recognize the young child with the new name. It is said that prior to the Naming Ceremony, the spirits are not able to see the face of the child. It is through this naming act that they look into the face of the child and recognize him as a living being. Thereafter, the Spirit World and all past relatives watch over and protect this child. They also prepare a place in the Spirit World that this living being can occupy when his life on Earth is at an end.

At this ceremony the parents of the child ask four women and four men to be sponsors for the child. It is a great honor to be asked to fill this position. After the child is given a name, each of the sponsors stand and proclaim a vow to support and guide this child in his development. In this way a provision is made by which the child will always be cared for.

Through this Naming Ceremony that was started by Original Man continuity is given to the lives of the people who would come to inhabit the Earth.

Today, we should use these ancient teachings to live our lives in harmony with the plan that the Creator gave us. We are to do these things if we are to be the natural people of the Universe.

Chapter 3

Original Man and His Grandmother — No-ko-mis

Boozhoo! It is good that you can join me in my home and listen to these old Ojibway teachings. I have much to tell you this time.

We ended our teaching last time when the Creator separated the paths of Original Man and wolf. After this happened, Original Man walked the Earth and observed the many miracles that were around him. He did not understand many of the things he saw so he asked these questions of his Grandfather, the Creator.

The Creator answered, "Across a vast lake lives your No-ko'-mis (Grandmother). She is not from the world you have walked; she has the wisdom of the spirits. Go to her lodge, for it is the elders who carry the knowledge of these things that you want to know."

Original Man began the search for Nokomis and came to a vast expanse of water. Try as he might, he could not figure out how to get to the far shore. He tried walking first in one direction and then the other so as to walk around the water, but there seemed to be no end to how far it extended.

Finally, he was so tired that he just sat down. The ba-nay'-she-ug' (birds) began to swoop about his head. "Fly! Fly across," they sang. "It's easy!" But Original Man looked at his arms and shook his head. He was not made for flying. The gi-gounh-nug' (fish) began to jump out of the water and tease him. "Swim! Swim across," they said. "It's fun!" But Original Man looked at his arms and legs. No, he was not made for swimming long distances either.

Original Man asked one of the fish, "Please swim across the water for me and see if my Grandmother does indeed live on the other side."

The fish swam away and was gone a long time.

Just about when Original Man was going to give up waiting, the fish returned.

"Your Grandmother does live across this water," he said. "She waits for you to come."

Original Man thought and thought about how he could get across the water. An idea came to him: he could float across on a log. He looked about and saw beavers working on a dam. He noticed how they cut the trees with their sharp teeth. Original Man found him a good ah-sin' (rock) and chipped it until it had a sharp edge. He tied it to a wooden handle with a piece of bark from Wee-goob-bee' (the basswood tree). With this new tool he cut down a tree and made a huge log from the tree.

Original Man dragged the log to the shore of the great water, shoved it in and jumped on top. It was hard to balance on the log and it rolled over, dunking Original Man and getting him all wet. He managed to swim back to shore pushing the log in front of him.

He thought about what he could do to make the log float better. He remembered once meeting a Gi'-tchie Man-a-meg' (whale) on one of his journeys around the Earth. As big as the whale was, he had no problem swimming and could easily hold himself upright in the water. With his wa-ga-kwud' (axe) Original Man shaped the bottom of the log just like the stomach of the whale. He even carved a seat into the top of the log for him to sit in.

Again, Original Man shoved the log into the water. This time he had no problem keeping the log upright, but soon he found himself just floating out in the water and not going any place. Soon, a chi-noo'-din (big wind) came up and tore at Original Man and his log. The winds blew him far away from his starting place, but they blew him further down the shore and not any closer to Nokomis.

Original Man knew he had to figure out something that would keep the log moving in the same direction. He remembered what a good swimmer Ah-mik' (beaver) was and that Ah-mik' had a wide, webbed foot and a flat tail. It took Original Man a long time to figure out what kind of wood would be best to use for the tool he had in mind. Finally, he selected a piece of hickory wood and with his axe he shaped an ah-bwi' (paddle) much like the foot and tail of Ah-mik'.

Once again, Original Man set out on his ba-ba'-ma-di-zi-win' (journey). He made good speed with his dugout log and his new paddle. But he never thought about having food or water along with him in the dugout. Pretty soon he started getting really hungry and thirsty. He tried drinking some of the water from the great water around him, but it tasted like zhe-wa-ta'-gun (salt). He was about to turn around and go back for some food and water when he realized that he was already very close to where he had started, and yet he had been paddling all day. You see, Original Man didn't understand how to paddle his dugout in a straight line. His whole day of paddling had taken him in a huge gi-we-tash'-skad (circle).

Original Man got back on shore and rested and thought about all the mistakes he had made. When he felt he was strong enough to set out on his fourth attempt to cross the great water, Original Man put Ah-say-ma' (Tobacco) in the water and asked the Creator for a safe and successful journey. All the animals gathered around him. The birds got together and sang a na-ga-moon' (song) to give him strength. Some of the animals cried for they were sad to see Original Man leave on such a long and dangerous journey. When he left, many of the birds flew

Original Man arrives at the lodge of No-kó-mis.

along with him as he paddled along. Many of the fish swam with him to keep him company.

Original Man had learned from his mistakes before and this time, he brought along a supply of food and water. This time, he kept sight of the Sun and the Moon and the Gi-way'-din ah-nung' (North Star) to help him travel in a straight line. He knew that there were certain big birds that could fly in perfectly straight lines for many miles, and he adjusted his paddling so that his journey might be like theirs.

Original Man had learned from all of this that he must use his environment to teach him things. The Creator had placed many lessons around him to teach him how to live in harmony with all of the Creation. He must use his mind—his thought and reasoning—to discover tools and better ways of doing things. He must be prepared to meet the challenges of each and every day.

Original Man paddled many days until, at last, he caught sight of the distant shore. When he came to the shore he found Nokomis in front of her lodge waiting for him.

She welcomed him and fed him and made him rest. While he was resting, Original Man began to notice that Nokomis had a very hard time providing for herself. She was too old to go hunting, and she could not get around well enough to make the things she needed for fishing. To feed herself, she had to scavenge around and eat from the kills that large animals like Mu-kwa' (bear) would leave. In be-boong' (winter), time was really hard for Nokomis. She could not even get water because she did not have an axe to cut a hole in the ice.

Original Man tried to make life better for Nokomis. He made her a beautiful wee-gi-wahm'

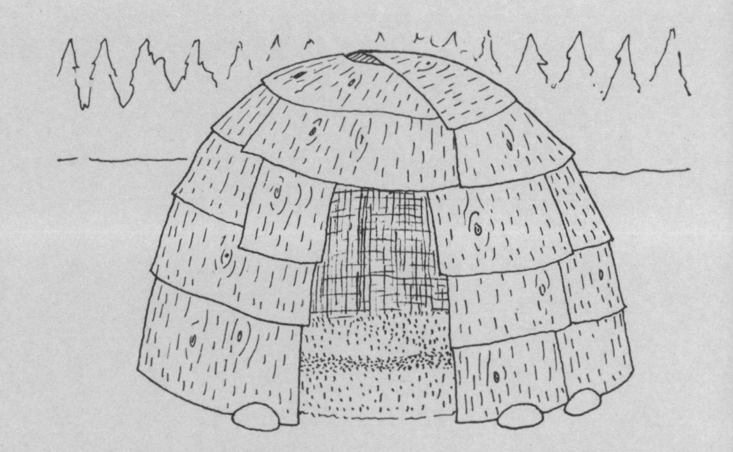

(lodge) with furnishings of the finest animal robes. With the birchbark he gathered, Nokomis made buckets and sealed them with be-gew' (sap or pitch) so that they could be used to haul water. With the Ah-gi-mak' (ash wood) he gathered, Nokomis made fine woven baskets for storing things. With the animal skins he provided, Nokomis made clothes for them. She made fine moccasins for their feet. She used woodashes and the brains of Wa-wa-shkesh'-shi (the deer) to make the leather soft. She used roots to give her dyes to make the clothes beautiful. She made Original Man a warm winter coat and a special bag so that he could carry with him all the things he needed on a journey. She embroidered beautiful flower designs on the bag with different colors of moose hair. From this bag came the bandolier bags that would later be used by Ojibway people. A bag like this came to be a sign of authority and its designs told about the owner.

As the seasons passed, Original Man and his Grandmother lived in harmony with the Earth. They picked berries, smoked fish, and dried meat all in accordance to the seasons. They stored much food to get ready for the approaching winter.

In the winter, as they would sit about in the wee-gi-wahm′ trying to stay warm, Nokomis would tell Original Man many stories. He had many questions for her about the mysteries of the Universe, and she answered them the best that she could.

He asked her, "How did the Universe begin and how did our Mother Earth come into being?"

Nokomis answered, "Grandson, first there was a void in the Universe. There was nothing to fill this emptiness but a sound. This sound was like that of a she-she-gwun′ (shaker)."

We use our shakers today in ceremonies to imitate that sound.

Nokomis continued, "Gitchie Manito was the first thought. He sent his thoughts out in every direction but they went on forever. There was nothing on which to bounce them back. Finally, Gitchie Manito had to call his thoughts back himself. The stars you see at night represent the trails of his thoughts.

"First, Gitchie Manito created Gee′-sis (Sun), so that he could have light to see. Then he tried creating other objects. One was the Wa-bun′ ah-nung′ (Morning Star) that tells us each day of

the approach of the Sun. Then, he tried to create a place on which to put life. One of his attempts turned out to be covered with a cloud. One was a rock full of heat. And one was covered with ice. On his fourth attempt he created Earth. He found it to be pleasing so he sent singers to it in the form of birds. The birds spread the seeds of new life.

"The Earth was arranged in the Universe so that Gee'-sis (Sun and Nee'-ba-gee-sis (Night Sun or Moon) would alternate walking in the sky keeping watch over the Creation. The Sun would keep watch during the day. The Moon would keep watch at night."

It is this movement of the Sun and the Moon that we imitate in ceremonies today when we pass things around in one direction.

Original Man learned from these experiences with his Grandmother that we should provide for our elders because they provide for us when we are young and need direction. They teach us all we need to know in order to live in this world. His work for Nokomis taught him that we must strive and work for things for the benefit of others who are close to us.

As winter drew to an end, Original Man grew more and more inquisitive. "Do I have a mother?" he asked Nokomis.

"Yes," she said. "There is no beauty like her." But she was reluctant to say more.

"Do I have a father?" he asked. "Yes, he is very close to perfection. He is second only to the Creator." But she would say no more.

Nokomis worked hard on a beautiful outfit for Original Man that she said he would wear when he would go to meet his father. She prepared him mentally and physically for all the things he would face in the future.

One day, his Grandmother told him about ish-skwa-day' (fire). She said, "There is a man who guards the Fire. You are to go to him and ask him for some of it so that we might be able to live better. Your journey will be hard and full of many tests. You must keep your heart and mind strong and stay true to the things I have taught you."

Original Man set out on his journey and first came to a vast expanse of water. Using the skills he had already learned, he quickly made a dugout and paddled across the water. Next, he came to a rocky, barren place which he crossed being careful not to fall. Original Man then came to a land of flat plains where the wind never stopped blowing. After he crossed this, he came to a very strange place. It looked as if there once was a zah-ga-e-gun' (lake) there. All the water had dried up and in its place was a sticky black substance that looked like the pitch Nokomis used to seal the birchbark buckets. To keep from sinking down into the pitch, Original Man tied a long, narrow piece of wood to the bottom of each foot. He tried walking with these, but he soon became stuck in the sticky black substance. Original Man thought long and hard about what he could do to get across this strange place. He finally tried greasing the bottom of the wooden boards with mush-ka-wuj'-i-be-mi-day· (deer fat or tallow). With this coating on the wood, he found he could slide along easily across the lake of pitch.

He at last came to the Firekeeper's lodge. He was surprised to see that the old man had a young and very beautiful daughter. For her, he felt a feeling that he had never felt before. He could not understand it. The Firekeeper was very stern with him. He said, "I have waited for you a long time. Your Grandfather, Gitchie Manito, told

me that you would be coming. Since that time, many others have tried to find this place. Many of them tried to trick me but I could tell that they were evil forces who wanted to use the fire I have in a bad way. You see, fire is a very special gift from the Creator. If you respect it and take care of it, it will take care of you and bring you warmth. But locked up in this goodness is also evil. If you neglect fire or use it in the wrong way, it could destroy the entire Creation. Many things in life have forces of good and evil locked up in them. Everytime you use fire you should remember that this is the same fire with which the Creator made the Sun. It is also the fire that the Creator put at the heart of your Mother Earth. You can use this fire to communicate with the Creator. You can use it to burn Tobacco and let its smoke carry your prayers to Gitchie Manito. This smoke will be like your thoughts as if you could see them.

With these teachings, the Firekeeper sent fire with Original Man to take back to Nokomis. Original Man put the fire in a small hollowed-out stone that Nokomis had sent with him. It was a long and difficult trip back to the lodge of Nokomis. Original Man had to be careful not to drop the fire on the pitch at the bottom of the dried-up lake or else he might start a fire so huge as to burn up the entire world. He had to be careful not to drop the fire as he crossed the rocky barren place. He had to be careful not to let the wind that never stopped blowing put the fire out when he crossed the plains. So also did he have to be careful when crossing the lake so that the water would not put out the fire.

Nokomis was very glad to see him when he approached her home. The fire he brought changed their lives drastically. Many animals that were good to eat offered themselves to Original Man. Some of the animals told of other animals that were good to eat.

Original Man's questions of Nokomis never ceased. He continued to press her for more information about his mother and father. She had a hard time holding back information as the curiosity of Original Man grew and grew. There was some knowledge that he was not quite ready for.

Nokomis was saddened a little because she knew her time with Original Man was drawing to a close. And yet she was a little happy because the Creator had told her that when she was finished in preparing Original Man for all he needed to know for his life on Earth, she would be sent to live in a special place. She would be sent to live with the Moon and watch over the changes in the Moon and the effects that these changes had on the Earth—things like the tides of the seas, the growth of plants, the actions of the animals, and more. Nokomis would also be charged with watching over all the women that would come to inhabit the Earth.

Original Man came to find out from Nokomis that his mother lived in the Wa-ba-noong′ (East) and that his father lived in the Ning-ga′-be-uh-noong′ (West). She even told him that he had a twin brother. Nokomis told him that there are things in life that one must go after and search for; they will not just come to a person. It is this way with knowledge. It is this way with many other things.

Original Man loved Nokomis very much. He was sad when he thought about leaving her. But he knew that there were many things in the world waiting for him to discover and learn from them. He was sure that Nokomis was now comfortable and well-provided for. He knew that the time was right for him to leave on yet another journey, this time to find his twin brother, his mother, and his father.

When Original Man was leaving Nokomis, she said to him, "Grandson, as I say goodbye to you I will call you Anishinabe. You are the first of the people that will be coming to live on this Earth. You are their ancestor. Therefore, they will also be called Anishinabe."

There are many important lessons for our lives hidden in these teachings about Original Man and his Grandmother. In the last part of the story Original Man and Nokomis were sad to see their time together come to an end, but they were happy in the beautiful things that lay ahead for them in the future. So is it with us and our life on this Earth. Of course, we would be sad at the thought of dying and leaving all our friends and the places we love. But we should be gald to realize that there are beautiful things that await us when we leave this life.

Think about all these teachings and the lessons they have for you.

Gi'-ga-wa-ba-min' na-gutch'! (See you later!)

Mishomis and Nokomis

Chapter 4

The Earth's First People

Boozhoo! It is good to see you again. It has been a long time since we talked. Since the teaching this time brings us to the first union between man and woman on the Earth, I would like to introduce someone very special to you. This is the woman who has added much meaning to my life. This is my woman Nokomis. She was given this name so as to honor the grandmothers all the way back to the Grandmother of Original Man. She will take up our story at this point.

Boozhoo! It is a great honor for me, Nokomis, to share with you the teaching of the Earth's first people.

When we left Original Man in our last chapter, he was leaving the lodge of his Grandmother to search for his mother, his father, and his twin brother. His Grandmother's last words were: "From now on I will call you 'Anishinabe.'" We will use this name for Original Man in this teaching.

Anishinabe sensed that his father lived in the West, in the land of the Ani-mi-keeg' (thunder beings). He traveled in this direction and used the movement of the Sun across the sky to guide him in a sure path. He had to travel around many lakes and cross many streams.

One night he made a camp for himself on the western shore of a large lake. The next morning he awoke to a beautiful na-ga-moon' (song) that seemed to float across the water of the lake. It came with the first rays of the new day's Sun in the East. No matter how hard Anishinabe looked, he could not make out who or what was making this beautiful song. He knew that he must continue on his journey to the West if he was to find his father, and yet this song was calling him back to the East. He struggled within himself as to what he should do. Finally, he decided to lay aside his search for his father and go to the East in search of the origin of the beautiful song.

Anishinabe made a canoe out of the bark of Wee'-gwas (the birch tree). It took him four days. Each day at sunrise and again at sundown, the song was repeated. At dawn of the fifth day, he stepped into the new jee-mon' (canoe). With his paddle he had carved from a hickory tree, Anishinabe headed straight across the water toward the rising Sun and the source of the beautiful song.

When the Sun was setting behind him in the western sky, Anishinabe arrived at the lake's eastern shore. There he saw a beautiful wee-gi-wahm' (lodge) made of saplings and birchbark. Baw-shki'-na-way' (smoke) was curling from the top of the lodge. Anishinabe beached his canoe and approached the singing lodge very carefully.

The door of the lodge faced the setting Sun. When he looked inside, his breath was taken away. The rays of the setting Sun were shining on the Firekeeper's Daughter! The feeling that came to him when he saw her with the Firekeeper returned, and he felt that he would burst with joy. Her beauty was overwhelming.

Her song stopped and she spoke: "Geen-wayzh'-in-da-ka-wa-ba-min'" (For a long time I have awaited your coming). "I have prepared this place for us."

Anishinabe looked around. He was in the most beautiful lodge he had ever seen. The floor was covered with furs of many animals. In the middle was a small fireplace that contained a warm fire.

Anishinabe was so full of happiness! It was clear to him now that the Creator had led him to this place and time. He realized that we often have to put our own plans and desires aside and follow the paths and opportunities that the Great Mystery puts in front of us.

Anishinabe and the Firekeeper's Daughter formed a we-di-gay'-win' (union or marriage) between man and woman that had never been formed on Mother Earth. Their union was complete and sacred in the eyes of Gitchie Manito. The zah-gi'-di-win' (love) that flowed between them was real and lasting.

Anishinabe remembered how beautiful the Firekeeper's Daughter was when he first saw her in the rays of the setting Sun. He decided then to help preserve this beauty in woman by taking upon himself the responsibility of doing the more strenuous things necessary for survival. Each of them molded their roles so that there was good food to eat and their home was both beautiful and comfortable. The most important thing that bound Anishinabe and the Firekeeper's Daughter together was the feeling of ma-na'-ji-win' (respect) that they shared between them. This foundation of respect was to be very important to guide future unions between men and women.

From the union of Anishinabe and the Firekeeper's Daughter, four gwe-wi-zayn'-sug' (sons) were born. They were raised with the teachings that Anishinabe had learned from his Grandmother and from his journeys around the Earth.

When these sons became young men, Anishinabe and the Firekeeper's Daughter sent each of them out on a long journey. Each son was sent to one of the Four Directions.

The son named Gi-way'-din traveled North. After traveling for a long time, he came to a place where a fire was burning in a fireplace in the Earth. Behind the fire sat an old man and a young and very beautiful woman.

Love and respect flowed between Anishinabe and the Firekeeper's Daughter.

"I am the Ish-kwan-day'-wi-nini (Doorman or Doorkeeper) of the North and this is my daughter," he said. "You are entering a land where Mother Earth is purified every year by deep snows. Even the big lakes and rivers in this land become frozen in Mother Earth's cycle. This is the home of the Bear Power. The Bear Power is the guardian of many secrets of how many diseases can be cured. There will be times when colored lights will come to the northern sky. They are called Wa-wa-sayg' (the Northern Lights). They come out to dance when the Bear Power is in its highest strength.

At this time, the Doorkeeper set fire to a long braid of grass. "This is We-skwu' ma-shko-seh' (Sweetgrass). It was the first plant to grow on Mother Earth. For this reason we braid this grass as if it were your Mother's hair. The smoke of this Sweetgrass will keep evil away from your home and will keep you safe on your travels."

This son traveled on and explored the beauty of the North. At times he would see the lights in the northern sky that the Doorkeeper had spoken of. He sensed that all the colors of the Universe came out and danced with the Star World.

The son named Wa-bun' traveled to the East. After walking for a long ways, he also came to a fireplace attended by an old man and a young woman.

"I am the Ish-kwan-day'-wi-nini of the East," he said. "The source of all knowledge. In your journey pay attention to all the things your Mother Earth has to teach you. I would like to teach you about Ah-say-ma' (Tobacco)." The Doorkeeper put some Tobacco in the fire. "The smoke from Tobacco will carry your thoughts into the Spirit World. Its smoke will be your visible thoughts. You must use Tobacco when you want to speak with your Grandfather, the Creator."

This son continued on his journey and at last came to a huge body of zhe-wi-ta'-ga-ni-bi' (salt water). There he would greet the Sun every morning as it rose over the water. The sunrise each morning seemed to this son to be truly a ma-ma-ka'-ji-win' (miracle) that told of the harmony of the entire Creation. It taught him that the flow of knowledge and wisdom in this world is endless and each day offers new learning experiences.

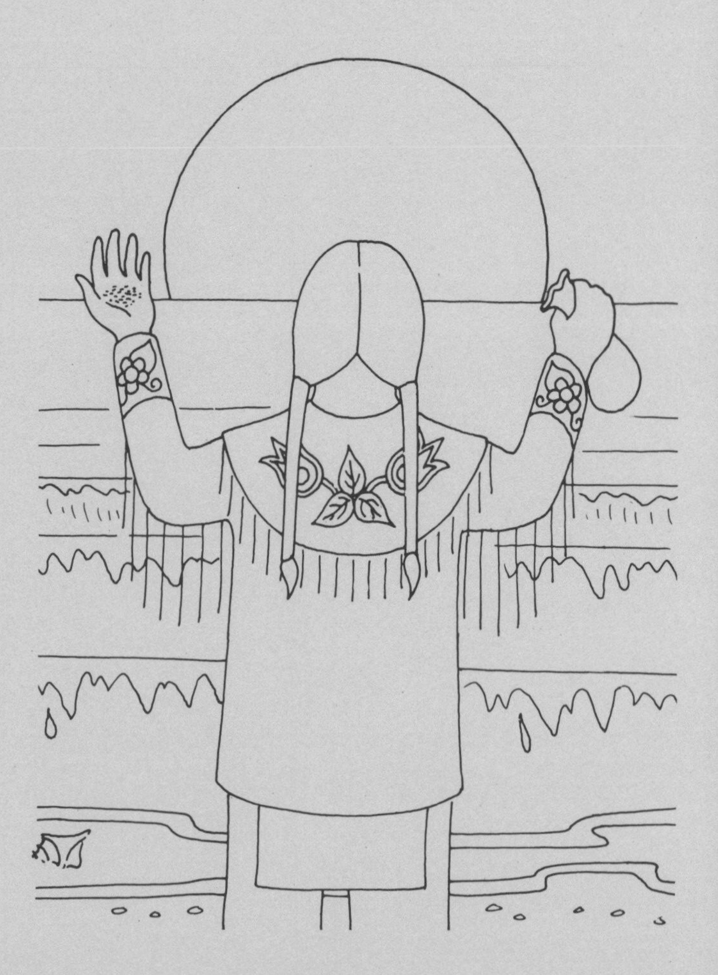

The son called Zha-wan′ traveled South and came upon a warm land where mild winds blew most of the year. The forests of this land were thick with trees and vines. The rivers were crooked and wound about over the land in huge loops. At last he came to a place where an old man and young and very beautiful woman seemed to be waiting for him by a fire.

The old man spoke: "I am the Ish-kwan-day′-wi-nini of the South. This is the land of birth and growth. This land is full of the songs of birds. Some of the birds come here every year to escape the hard winters of the North. When winter is over, the birds fly from this fertile land and carry with them the gi-ti-gay′-mi-non′ (seeds) of life. In this way life is replenished in each of the Four Directions."

The Doorkeeper put a handful of something into the fire. It popped and cracked and gave off a sweet and medicinal smell. "This is Gi-shee-kan′-dug (Cedar)," he said. "Use this to purify your body from disease and to protect you from evil."

This son left the Doorkeeper and his daughter and continued his journey through the land of the South.

The son named Ning-ga′-be-un traveled west. After he had gone a ways he found his journey was blocked by chi′-wa-ji-wan′ (huge mountains) that were covered with rocks, forests, and meadows. Some of these mountains were so high that there was very little air to breathe and snow covered the ground in places all through the year. After he crossed the mountains he came upon a land in which there was no water to be found anywhere. The days were gi-zhi-day′ (hot) and the nights were gi-si-naw′ (cold). This son was amazed that there were types of plants and animals that were able to live in this dry land. He hurried on to find more forests and mountains. At last he too came to a place where an old man and a young woman waited by a fire.

The old man said, "I am the Ish-kwan-day′-wi-nini of the West. I would like to give you Mush′-ko-day-wushk′ (Sage). As he said this, he sprinkled a silver-looking leaf on the fire. The smoke had a powerful smell. "The smoke of this plant can be used to purify your body and surroundings and keep you in good health. This land of the West is the place of the setting Sun. It is beyond this setting Sun where the gee-baw′-ug (spirits) have their home. It is to this world that all spirits must travel after their life is over on Earth. You must be careful not to fear these spirits or the path of the departed. Instead, appreciate the joys of what life you are blessed with on this Earth."

This son continued on his way and wandered through the land of the West. He also came to a great water that tasted of salt. The setting Sun seemed to represent the completion of life's cycle.

After the four sons had explored these lands they each returned to the doorways of these regions and asked the Doorkeepers there for permission to take their daughters and make homes for themselves. Each of these couples found the happiness of we-di-gay'-win'. They formed circles that were strong and unbroken. These circles represented the harmony and fullness that can come when man and woman join their lives together in a sacred way.

The unions of each of these new families were blessed with nee-jaw-ni-sug' (children). It was not many years before these children grew up to travel about and establish families of their own. The tribes began to grow. There were only a few people living here and there, but in each of the Four Directions there were the sounds of hunting, singing, laughter, lodgemaking, teachings, and all things necessary for life to develop in a good way.

Life in some places was hard for the people. It is said that there was once a time when ice came from the North and covered much of the Earth. In some villages certain men would run for long distances over the ice and snow to communicate with other villages and to find herbs, medicines and plant foods that existed on patches of Earth here and there. The task of the runners was made harder by the fact that the great sheets of ice on the Earth gradually shifted so that the patches of plant foods and medicines changed from time to time. These people that lived on the vast expanses of ice and snow were called the Oh-kwa-ming'-i-nini-wug' (Ice People). The men that gave of themselves as runners were a special breed of men. Because of their sacrifices to the people, they were given a high place of honor.

It has been told through the ages that once a group of runners found a litter of wolf pups out in the frozen wilderness and brought them back to their village. It was thought that the pups could be raised as dogs and cooked and eaten if ever the people were in desperate need of food.

The pups, though, wanted to seek another way to become useful to the people. When they grew up, they started going out to meet the exhausted runners and lead them home. On one occasion, one of the strongest dogs spoke to the runners and instructed them in the making of a zhoosh-ku'-da-bahn (sled). This dog told them of how six dogs could be harnessed to a sled that would take a man much faster and further over the snow. They could expand their communication with other villages and their food gathering expeditions.

This linkage of man and dog was very important because it combined the intelligence of man with intuition of the dog. If a man was to get lost in the wilderness, his dogs could lead him back home. This joining of man and dog was also important because it continued the teaching of the close bond that once existed between Anishinabe and the wolf in their journeys around the Earth.

The number seven, obtained by joining the six dogs to the one man with the sled, was to become a very special number to the Earth's people as their spiritual ways developed.

No matter how hard life was for the Earth's first people, every day was recognized as the bringer of beautiful experiences and new lessons to be learned from the surrounding world. The o-day-nah-wayn'-sun' (small villages) of the people grew. New villages were formed here and there across Mother Earth.

I will end this teaching here. Mishomis and I will continue next time with the stories that have been passed down to us of how life developed for these first people of the Earth.

Mishomis and Nokomis use the Wee-gwas'(birchbark) scrolls to remember the details of the Ojibway teachings. They have prepared to offer Tobacco in thanksgiving for your joining them.

Chapter 5

The Great Flood

Boozhoo! We are glad that you could join us for some more of the Ojibway teachings. In our last time together, Nokomis told of how the first people of the Earth developed from the union of Anishinabe (Original Man) and the Firekeeper's Daughter. Although life was often hard for them, for many years the first people lived together in harmony with all of the Creation.

I regret to say that this harmonious way of life on Earth did not last forever. Men and women did not continue to give each other the respect needed to keep the Sacred Hoop of marriage strong. Families began quarreling with each other. Finally villages began arguing back and forth. People began to fight over hunting grounds. Brother turned against brother and began killing each other.

It greatly saddened the Creator, Gitchie Manito, to see the Earth's people turn to evil ways. It seemed that the entire Creation functioned in harmony except for the people who were the last to be placed there. For a long time Gitchie Manito waited hoping that the evil ways would cease and that brotherhood, sisterhood, and respect for all things would again come to rule over the people.

When it seemed that there was no hope left, Gitchie Manito decided to purify the Earth. He would do this with water. The water came like a mush-ko'-be-wun' (flood) upon the Earth. The flood came so fast that it caught the entire Creation off guard. Most all living things were drowned immediately, but some of the animals were able to keep swimming, trying to find a small bit of land on which to rest. Some of the birds were caught in the air and had to keep flying in order to stay alive.

The purification of the Earth with water appeared to be complete. All the evil that had built up in the hearts of the first people had been washed away.

But how could life on Mother Earth begin anew?

There are many Ojibway teachings that refer to a man named "Way-na-boo'-zhoo." Some people have actually referred to Anishinabe or Original Man as Waynaboozhoo. Most of the elders agree that Waynaboozhoo was not really a man but was a spirit who had many adventures during the early years of the Earth. Some people say that

Waynaboozhoo and the animals on the giant log

Waynaboozhoo provided the link through which human form was gradually given to the spiritual beings of the Earth. Everyone agrees that Waynaboozhoo had many human-like characteristics. He made mistakes at times just like we do. But he also learned from his mistakes so that he could accomplish things and become better at living in harmony with the Earth. These things that Waynaboozhoo learned were later to become very useful to Indian people. He has been looked upon as kind of a hero by the Ojibway. These "Waynaboozhoo Stories" have been told for many years to children to help them grow in a balanced way.

In our teachings from now on, we will use the name "Waynaboozhoo" to refer to the spirit of Anishinabe or Original Man.

The teaching about how a new Earth was created after the Great Flood is one of the classic Waynaboozhoo Stories. It tells of how Waynaboozhoo managed to save himself by resting on a chi-mi-tig' (huge log) that was floating on the vast expanse of water that covered Mother Earth. As he floated along on this log, some of the animals that were able to keep swimming came to rest on the log. They would rest for a while and then let another swimming animal take their place. It was the same way with the winged creatures. They would take turns resting on the log and flying. It was through this kind of sacrifice and concern for one another that Waynaboozhoo and large group of birds and four-leggeds were able to save themselves on the giant log.

They floated for a long time but could gain no sight of land. Finally, Waynaboozhoo spoke to the animals.

"I am going to do something," he said. "I am going to swim to the bottom of this water and grab a handful of Earth. With this small bit of Earth, I believe we can create a new land for us to live on with the help of the Four Winds and Gitchie Manito."

So Waynaboozhoo dived into the water. He was gone a long time. Some of the animals began to cry for they thought that Waynaboozhoo must have drowned trying to reach the bottom.

At last, the animals caught sight of some bubbles of air, and finally, Waynaboozhoo came to the top of the water. Some of the animals helped him onto the log. Waynaboozhoo was so out of breath that he could not speak at first. When he regained his strength, he spoke to the animals.

"The water is too deep . . . I never reached the bottom . . . I cannot swim fast enough or hold my breath long enough to make it to the bottom."

All the animals on the log were silent for a long time. Mahng (the loon) who was swimming alongside the log was the first to speak.

"I can dive under the water for a long ways, for that is how I catch my food. I will try to dive to the bottom and get some of the Earth in my beak."

The loon dived out of sight and was gone a long time. The animals felt sure he had drowned, but the loon floated to the top of the water. He was very weak and out of breath.

"I couldn't make it," he gasped. "There appears to be no bottom to this water."

Next, Zhing-gi-biss' (the helldiver) came forth.

"I will try to swim to the bottom," he said. "I am known for diving to great depths."

The helldiver was gone for a very long time. When the animals and Waynaboozhoo were about to give up hope, they saw the helldiver's body come floating to the top. He was unconscious and Waynaboozhoo had to pull him onto the log and help him regain his breath. When the helldiver came to, he spoke to all the animals on the log.

"I am sorry my brothers and sisters. I, too, could not reach the bottom although I swam for a long ways straight down."

Many of the animals offered themselves to do the task that was so important to the future of all life on Earth. Zhon-gwayzh' (the mink) tried but could not make it to the bottom. Ni-gig' (the otter) tried and failed. Even Mi-zhee-kay' (the turtle) tried but was unsuccessful.

All seemed hopeless. It appeared that the water was so deep that no living thing could reach its bottom. Then a soft, muffled voice was heard.

"I'll try," it said softly.

At first, no one could see who it was that spoke. The little Wa-zhushk' (muskrat) stepped forth.

"I'll try," he said again.

Some of the animals laughed and poked each other. The helldiver jeered, "If **I** couldn't make it how can **he** expect to do any better?"

Waynaboozhoo spoke, "Hold it everyone! It is not our place to judge the merits of another; that task belongs to the Creator. If little muskrat wants to try, I feel we should let him."

The muskrat dived down and disappeared from view. He was gone for such a long time that Waynaboozhoo and all the animals on the log were certain that muskrat had given up his life in trying to reach the bottom.

The muskrat was able to make it to the bottom of the water. He was already very weak from lack of air. He grabbed some Earth in his paw and with every last bit of strength he could muster, muskrat pushed away from the bottom.

One of the animals on the log caught sight of muskrat as he floated to the water's surface. They pulled his body onto the log. Waynaboozhoo examined the muskrat.

"Brothers and sisters," Waynaboozhoo said. "Our little brother tried to go without air for too long. He is dead." A song of mourning and praise was heard over all the water as Wa-zhushk''s spirit passed to the next world.

Waynaboozhoo spoke again, "Look! Muskrat has something in his paw. It is closed tight around something." Waynaboozhoo carefully pried open muskrat's tiny paw. All the animals gathered around trying to see. Muskrat's paw opened and there, in a little ball, was a piece of Earth. All the animals cheered! Muskrat had sacrificed his life so that life could begin anew on the Earth.

Waynaboozhoo took the piece of Earth from the muskrat's paw. At that moment, Mi-zhee-kay' (the turtle) swam forward and said, "Use my back to bear the weight of this piece of Earth. With the help of the Creator, we can make a new Earth."

Waynaboozhoo put the piece of Earth on the turtle's back. All of a sudden the noo-di-noon' (winds) began to blow. The wind blew from each of the Four Directions. The tiny piece of Earth on the turtle's back began to grow. Larger and larger it became, until it formed a mi-ni-si' (island) in the water. Still the Earth grew but still the turtle bore its weight on his back.

Waynaboozhoo began to sing a song. All the animals began to dance in a circle on the growing island. As he sang, they danced in an ever-widening circle. Finally, the winds ceased to blow and the waters became still. A huge island sat in the middle of the great water.

Today, traditional Indian people sing special songs and dance in a circle in memory of this event. Indian people also give special honor to our brother, the turtle. He bore the weight of the new Earth on his back and made life possible for the Earth's second people.

To this day, the ancestors of our brother, the muskrat, have been given a good life. No matter that marshes have been drained and their homes destroyed in the name of progress, the muskrats continue to multiply and grow. The Creator has made it so that muskrats will always be with us because of the sacrifice that our little brother made for all of us many years ago when the Earth was covered with water. The muskrats do their part today in remembering the Great Flood; they build their homes in the shape of the little ball of Earth and the island that was formed from it.

We hope you have found this teaching about the Great Flood to be meaningful. Nokomis and I have much more that we would like to share with you that leads up to our life today as Indian people.

Bi-wa-ba-mi'-shi-nam' me-na-wah'! (Come see us again!) Migwetch!

Chapter 6

"Waynaboozhoo and the Search for His Father"

In our last chapter, we learned of how Waynaboozhoo and all the animals on the giant log survived the flood that purified the Earth of all disharmony. The little muskrat gave his life in diving down into the water and bringing up a small piece of Earth. The turtle bore the weight of this piece of Earth on his back and, through the Creator, it was transformed into a huge island. This is the way that life began for the Earth's second people.

When Waynaboozhoo saw that his task was done, he rejoined his woman, the Firekeeper's Daughter. She had been given a place by the Creator to make her home for all time. That place was in the Wa-bun-noong' (East). The fire of her lodge burned brightly and announced each day the coming of the Morning Star.

He spoke with the Firekeeper's Daughter: "For many years I have been doing task after task that has been set before me. I have had to put aside my own wishes and desires. There are still questions that I have not answered for myself. I have never seen my own mother and father! I must find my father. I must know what happened to my mother and my twin brother. It is a thing I must do."

The Firekeeper's Daughter was torn with her own desire to have Waynaboozhoo remain with her in their lodge. But, at the same time, she recognized that Waynaboozhoo must accomplish these tasks before he could really be a full man.

Her feelings about Waynaboozhoo's leaving reminded her of the teachings that the Creator had given her and Waynaboozhoo when they were blessed with children. Their responsibility was to care for them and prepare them for the work of the Creator. They were never to feel that they owned their children or that the work or desires of their children should be as their own. She remembered the ache in her heart when she saw her children leave their home to go to each of the Four Directions. She was proud that her children represented the beginnings of the first people of the Earth.

The Firekeeper's Daughter realized that she must give Waynaboozhoo the same freedom that they had given their children to seek out their path in the Creator's plan. She knew that the Creator's plan would not lead Waynaboozhoo out of her life; their marriage commitment was sacred and lasting for all time.

The Creator has a plan for each of us. No one — husband or wife, mother or father, friend or foe — should prevent a person from fulfilling that plan. To do so would deny our sacred existence on this Earth. Life in comparison would be shallow and meaningless. This does not mean that we can turn our back on our loved ones when they needs us. To live a harmonious life, one must reach a gwa-yah-koo'-shka-win' (balance) between opposing forces. Respect for our brothers, sisters, and loved ones should also guide our path in life.

Waynaboozhoo returned to the Earth and continued his journey. He started where a great body of salt water seemed to stretch away forever into the East. Waynaboozhoo traveled west just as he had before when his journey was interrupted by the beautiful song of the Firekeeper's Daughter. Somehow he knew that in the land of the Ning-ga'-be-uh-noong' (West) he would find his father.

As he rested each night, he watched the Moon as she went through her changes. The movements of the Moon across the sky seemed sacred to Waynaboozhoo. First, she appeared as a small, cresent-shaped sliver in the sky. Slowly she revealed half of a circle of light. Slowly she revealed her full face to Waynaboozhoo. He was to pass down to the Earth's people knowledge and respect for the Moon's phases. Each face she wore was to become an important measure of time for the Earth's people. The Moon and her phases would reveal to the people important times of great power, planting, meditating and fasting.

One night, the Moon rose as a solid circle of light in the eastern sky. Waynaboozhoo was breathless at her beauty and power. As the Moon flooded the Earth with light, Waynaboozhoo was flooded with thoughts of his Grandmother. He wondered if she was able to get enough food and stay warm on these cold nights.

Suddenly, the manitou-wa'-bi (spirit) of his Grandmother spoke to him. It seemed as though she was speaking from the Moon. She told Waynaboozhoo how the Creator had rewarded her by giving her the Moon as an eternal home. She told him how it was her purpose to watch over the i-kway'-wug (women) of the Earth and guide their lives. She told him of the powers of the Moon and how the Moon was symbolic of womanhood and the cycle of oon-da'-di-zoo-win' (birth). She explained that woman was used by the Creator to cast the light of knowledge on man just as the Moon casts its light on the Earth. Alone, man is backwards and undeveloped. He needs the light that woman gives to make him whole.

In closing, his Grandmother said to him, "The Moon, as a woman, is the counterpart to the Sun. At some time in your journey you will be given a sign by the Sun that will explain this relationship further to you."

Waynaboozhoo wondered what his Grandmother meant by the sign that the Sun was going to show him. He was happy that his Grandmother was safe and that her life had been fulfilled. He realized that he did not have to take care of her anymore. He knew, too, that she would watch over and guide him on his quest.

Waynaboozhoo continued his journey to the West. He came to a land of great may-gway-yawk' (forests), beautiful rivers and deep blue lakes. Once at a river between two of the great lakes he stopped at a huge waterfall. Kitchi-ka'-be-kong (Great Falls) he called it. He stayed there a long time gazing into the falls and thinking about the journey that was in front of him. The great falls was a place of great power and reminded Waynaboozhoo of the power of water

to give and take life. He seemed to gain strength from the roar of the great falls. This place was to become an important landmark for the Anishinabe people that followed Waynaboozhoo.

As he continued on his journey he found that the going was hard. There were many rivers and lakes to cross. He counted five great lakes in this region whose waters stretched away for many, many miles. Gi-chi-gu'-mee or huge freshwater seas he called them. He found ma-no'-min (wild rice) growing in the westernmost lakes and somehow he knew that this land was one day going to become home to the Anishinabe.

Waynaboozhoo came to a huge river, the biggest he had ever seen. He sensed that this river was a vital part in all the waterways of the land in which he was traveling. He knew that this river must always be respected and even appeased because it held great power. This river was that which gave life to much land in all directions. It also received many rivers that nourished and removed wastes from many other lands. It was the father of waters.

The river seemed impossible to cross. Its waters were deep and fast. All at once, the waters of the river spoke to Waynaboozhoo.

"I am Michi-zee-bee', 'the greatest river.' What brings you to my shore?"

Waynaboozhoo told the river that he was traveling west to find his father and that he needed to cross over to the other shore.

The river flowed on.

Finally, Waynaboozhoo thought of the Ah-saymah' (Tobacco) that he carried with him. He sprinkled some of the Tobacco in the water as an offering to the river.

The river spoke: "I can sense that you are determined to continue your journey no matter what I tell you. I can see that you are sincere in your purpose. I will show you a place to cross my waters."

Even today when Indian people come to a river that they must cross they offer Tobacco and ask the Great Mystery that they might be shown a place where they could cross safely.

After Waynaboozhoo was shown safely across the water, the river spoke again: "There is yet another river to the west who is the princess of all rivers. She is called O-gi-ma-kway'-zee-bee'. Together, we are among the main arteries of Mother Earth. We help to drain and purify her blood. You must speak with her as a boy might speak to his aunt or grandmother. I wish you well on your quest to find your father. If and when you find your father, tell him that in the summertime when I like to doze and take long naps, his rumbling and stomping are very disturbing. Now be gone! I have to be on my way for it takes seven years to complete my journey to the sea and back again!"

Waynaboozhoo continued walking to the West. The land leveled out into a huge mush-ko-dayng' (plain). He could see no end to these great plains. He noticed, though, that even in the seeming barrenness of the plains and prairies, they were still teeming with life, songs, and vitality.

One especially hot day on the prairie, Waynaboozhoo sensed that something was strange. The animals around him ceased their scurrying about for food and became silent. All of a sudden, a shadow began to creep over the face of the Sun. Waynaboozhoo became frightened as the shadow grew and the light on the Earth became less and less. Finally, the Earth appeared as if it were night. But then, with a flash of light, the Sun started to reappear and the light gradually returned to the earth.

Waynaboozhoo remembered the time that his Grandmother's spirit talked with him from her home on the Moon. She had told him that the

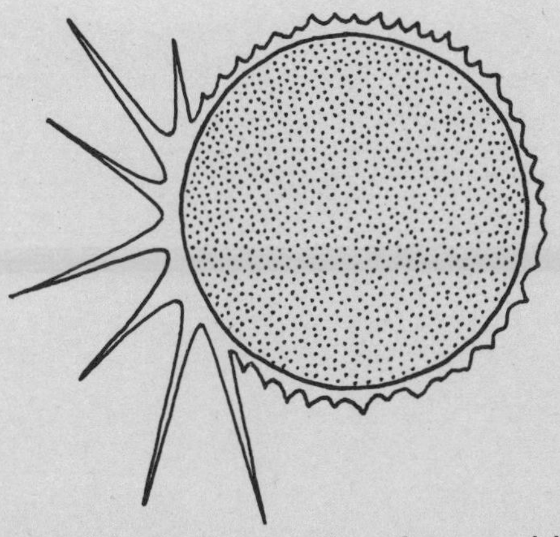

Sun would give him a sign that would explain the relationship between the Sun and Moon.

Waynaboozhoo knew that he had just been given that sign and that this time of darkness symbolized the time that the Moon, as woman, and the Sun, as man, would come together and honor their relationship. This sign would come to remind all women and men of their responsibility to each other even in the midst of all their earthly tasks.

Also this sign should be interpretted as a testimony to the harmony of the entire Creation, of how the stars, moons, and planets are placed in a sacred order with a sacred purpose. The Sun never fails to give the Earth its warmth and light, but just for this moment the Sun is given a rest, a rest that should remind us that we cannot take the Sun or any part of the Creation for granted.

Waynaboozhoo came to another great river and he knew this to be the O-gi-ma-kway′-zee-bee′. In talking with her he realized that each and all things have twins and that the two great rivers he had encountered were the pair that worked together in this part of the world. When he had crossed, the river told him, "Respect all, fear none! Tell your father that when he rants and raves he causes the torrents to send great amounts of water down through my banks and makes me swell up and become upset and cranky!"

Away to the West Waynaboozhoo began to hear a great rumbling noise like thunder. He could see a huge cloud holding close to the Earth and coming his way. He feared that this was still another obstacle coming to prevent him from continuing his journey.

As the cloud got closer, Waynaboozhoo was surprised and frightened to see that the cloud was being caused by many huge animals running straight at him. The Earth began to tremble. He finally recognized them as the Mush-ko-dayn′ Bi-shi-kee′ (buffalo) he had seen once on a journey long before he had found the lodge of his Grandmother.

The buffalo stopped just in front of him. A huge wall they made. Waynaboozhoo sat and waited. Day upon day he waited. He was getting very hungry. Finally, one of the buffalo stepped forward. He was huge and powerful. He was proud. He spoke to Waynaboozhoo.

"I see that we cannot dissuade you from continuing your journey. Since you seem determined, I will walk beside you and guide you for a ways. Across these plains the winds blow very strong. Sometimes the winds bring snow that covers the Earth and can cause you to become blind and lost forever. Only I am able to survive. If this happens stand at my side and I shall protect you. I will do this because I am one of your oldest brothers. I know that you are searching for your father. Tell him that I send greetings but it is not funny when he rumbles and sends lightning shafts among the buffalo cows. They get frightened and sometimes run for days. I have to run after them and catch them and make them stop.

It takes a long time and it is tiring. I don't like running all that much. Tell him to ease up a bit! I know he likes to tease me and that he laughs when I have to run after my wives. Tell him this for me!"

The giant buffalo told Waynaboozhoo many more things as they walked along. He told Waynaboozhoo how each being on the Earth has a purpose to fulfill in life and that we as brothers and sisters must seek to understand and respect that purpose. The buffalo advised Waynaboozhoo: "When you approach the land of your Father, you should call to him from a great distance and ask him to come meet with you. Do not be disappointed if he does not come. If you can complete this task of coming to an understanding with your father, then your act will prevent conflict and warfare between father and son for many ages to come. I must leave you now but I will give you a gift. In the future if you ever need me, I will help you as an older brother should. I will be waiting in the land of the West."

Waynaboozhoo did not understand all of what the buffalo had said to him but he kept the conversation with him. He knew that he would come to understand it some day.

Waynaboozhoo could see huge mountains looming up on the horizon to the West. With a feeling that weighed heavy on his heart he continued on. He saw rolling clouds coming at him over the mountains. Again he could hear rumbling in the West.

As he walked, Waynaboozhoo noticed the change in the terrain as he moved from the plains into the foothills of the mountains ahead. He marveled at the changes in the grass, flowers, shrubs, trees, and rocks. He was amazed that no matter how rugged the land became, there were always different types of flowers to greet him. There was also a change in the kinds of animals that roamed the land. In some places there seemed to be an abundance of the hooved ones: the deer, elk, and sheep. He knew from teachings he had heard that he was approaching the range of Chi'ga-zha-gayns' (the big cat).

The clouds from the West came closer and closer until they were right overhead. The rumbling got louder and louder. At last the rumbling reached a roar and spoke to Waynaboozhoo.

"We are the Ani-mi-keeg' (little thunders). How is it that you are so bold to appear in this land?"

The little thunders would not even listen to Waynaboozhoo's reply. They continued to shout at Waynaboozhoo as he pushed on into the West. They followed him up into the mountains. In the valleys between the great rocky peaks, the little thunders would race at Waynaboozhoo and tear at him with their wind. Waynaboozhoo pushed on even though the air became so thin that he could hardly breathe. As he climbed he was surprised to find areas of unmelted snow

The giant buffalo guided Waynaboozhoo across the plains.

even though it was summer. At last the little thunders seemed to give up in their attempt to turn him back and disappeared in the West.

As Waynaboozhoo continued traveling in the mountains, he pondered all that he saw. He looked up into the sky and noticed that the clouds were fleecy white, pure, and cold just like the snow at the tops of the mountains. He knew that high above the Earth there must be layers of air and elements that he had no name for. Nonetheless, he knew that something was up there that held it all together. He noticed too that high in the sky, clouds would be blown very fast while on the ground there would be no wind. At times, he would feel the wind blow in one direction and look up to find the clouds to be blowing the opposite direction. He was truly surrounded with evidence of the Great Mystery.

High in the sky, swooping and wheeling in the drafts of air, flew Mi-gi-zi' (the eagle). His scream announced his presence and foretold his approach. To this day we are told that there is an eagle that sits on a high place between this world and the next. He tells the Creator of the approach of the Anishinabe who have finished their earthly time.

While Waynaboozhoo was working his way through a particularly rough stretch of huge rocks and tangled brush, he heard, coming from just ahead, the most terrible roar that can be imagined. As he rounded a large boulder, he found himself face to face with a huge Mi-sa'-be Mu-kwa' (grizzly bear). For a moment, he felt his fear almost give way to sheer terror. Only with the greatest effort was he able to stand his ground. He looked at the huge bear and felt a massive power that seemed to come from his eyes. He noticed his powerful arms and huge paws with their long, sharp claws. These claws would later become a symbol worn by men that would attest to physical bravery. This mark of bravery would be achieved by few. This badge would symbolize Waynaboozhoo's overcoming his fear and controlling his terror. It is important that this be remembered for if we do not overcome our fear, then terror will come to control us.

Mi-sa'-be spoke in a powerful voice: "What do you want here? Do not put your tracks on this territory that I have been instructed to guard and care for. Go back! Go away!"

Waynaboozhoo replied, "Older brother, I come not to put my tracks on your ground or to violate your territory. I only ask that I be allowed to pass that I, too, may be able to fulfill the wishes of the Creator."

With that, Waynaboozhoo reached for his Tobacco, placed an offering on the ground, and spoke again: "I wish not to mar the beauty of the Earth or to disturb my brother's purpose. Allow me to pass."

Mi-sa'-be was a little confused. He did not expect Waynaboozhoo to remain so calm. He was used to scaring the daylights out of whomever he pleased. He felt that Waynaboozhoo was

worthy of knowledge. He spoke again: "I am **one** of your older brothers. There is yet one older than I whom you shall meet if he so desires. It is my purpose to be a helper to the Gi-chie' Mu-kwa' (Great Bear) who guards the Gi-way'-di-noong' (North). You see, Gi-chie' Mu-kwa' must care for the ice and snow in the North so that it will not melt so fast. If the ice and snow were all to melt, the Earth would be covered with water. The Creator saw this when he made a place for life to be. The world cannot be all water and it cannot be all ice and snow. As the water circulates on the Earth, it is part of its cycle to freeze as ice for a time. After a while, it will melt and flow again.

"So it is the Great Bear who cares for this part of the Creation. He does this by roaming and, at times, dancing in the North. He leaves his tracks in the ice and snow. When the Creator looks down this way and sees the tracks, he knows that his servant is still following his original instructions."

Waynaboozhoo asked: "But brother, how is it that you are here in these mountains?"

Mi-sa'-be answered: "My cousin, the Great Bear, knows that here too there is ice and snow to be cared for. He asked me to come here as his helper to put down my tracks. Someday, those people who will come behind you will look for the tracks of their ancestors. Someday, they will almost lose them. And, too, someday they will search for my tracks. I wonder if they will find them?

"It is time for you to go. I know the purpose of your journey. There are only certain places that you can cross these mountains. I will show you the way. Tell your father that I send him greetings and that I am proud he has such a son. Bravery is a good thing to know, but it must be cared for and tempered with reason. Otherwise, bravery can be a foolish thing. Also tell your father that I can hear him laughing when the snow suddenly slides down the mountain when I least expect it. It is not funny to suddenly find yourself tumbling down the mountain and losing your breath. Go now! We shall not meet often, but when you need me I shall answer."

After his encounter with Mi-sa'-be, Waynaboozhoo came to a greater understanding of the high peaks and the ice and snow. The sudden wind storms and blizzards did not catch him by surprise. He learned to respect the great and strange place of the mountains. He knew that man was not meant to live here. This is a special, awesome place where the wind sings its greatest songs. This is a place where silence is most powerful. With this knowledge and respect, Waynaboozhoo passed through the mountains peacefully.

When Waynaboozhoo at last descended from the mountains he was confounded to see yet another expanse of flat land stretched out in front of him. Once he was on the prairies, the little thunders came in force in a last attempt to turn Waynaboozhoo back. They pelted him with gi-mi-wun′ (rain) and mi-kwa′-mi-wun′ (hail) and tore at him with their winds. Waynaboozhoo struggled on. The little thunders even tried coming at Waynaboozhoo from different directions in an attempt to throw him off course. But as he walked, Waynaboozhoo kept the East at his back. The little thunders never sounded there; somehow they were forbidden to do so.

Then almost at once, most of the little thunders raced off into the West. They went to tell the father of Waynaboozhoo that his long-awaited son was approaching.

Waynaboozhoo walked on and came to still another range of mountains not quite as tall as those he had left behind. He journeyed without resting until he came to a forest of Ween-di-goo′-mi-tig′ (giant trees). They were so tall that he could not even see their tops. He could walk no further. Underneath the giant trees, Waynaboozhoo made camp. He built a fire and rested. As he lay there, it sounded as though the trees were whispering to him: "Why do you want to do such a thing as this journey you have set out on? It is crazy. It is crazy!"

Waynaboozhoo dozed off but soon awoke with a start as if someone or something had prodded him. He looked around slowly. Even though he did not see anything, he knew he was not alone. Suddenly, he noticed that just out of his direct eyesight was a being—a huge, dark figure with red eyes that peered out of a shadowy face.

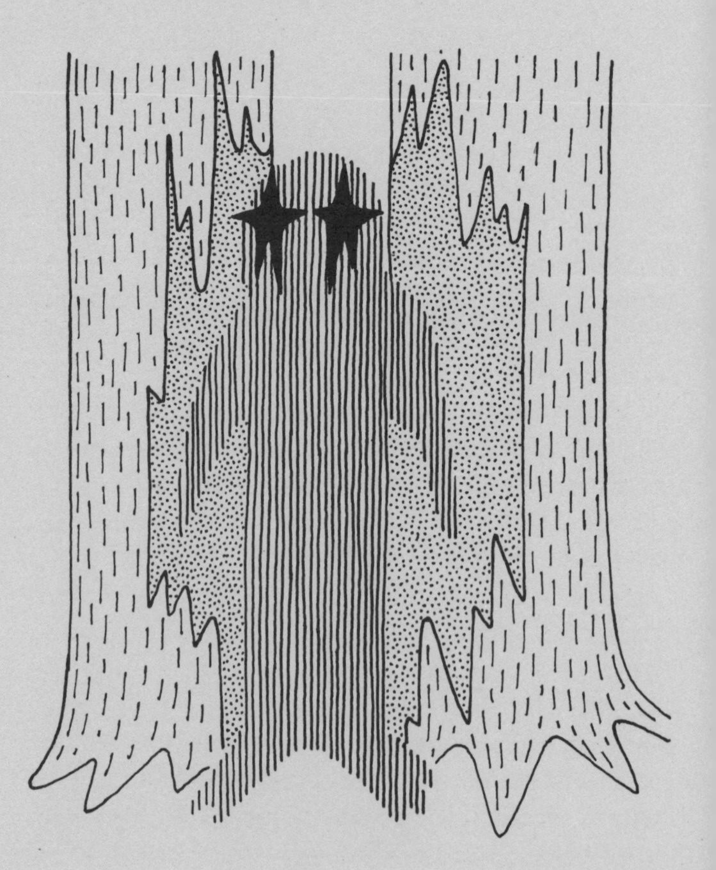

Again he felt his fear rising to an uncontrollable level. He wanted to run. He thought fleetingly of defending himself . . . of **fighting** . . . but violence was unknown to the world at that time. He was able to control both his fear and terror but still he felt a new, strange sensation. What was this strange feeling that possessed him? For the first time in many years, violence was evident on the Earth. But with Waynaboozhoo it was only a thought. He was able to put it aside. Violence, which is the twin of peace must always be secondary and subservient to peace just as it was with Waynaboozhoo.

The shadowy being spoke: "I am Bug-way'-ji-nini (wildman). Some of the people who follow you will know me as Sasquatch or Yeti, but they will seldom see me. It will be forbidden for them to look into my eyes. Some will not ever know of me. Many will not believe that I exist. I am your oldest brother!

"I have been with you on your journey. I have been ahead of you at times and behind you at times. Sometimes I have watched you walk by. The Creator sent me here to guide and care for those who become lost. I am to watch over those who go into the forests, swamps, hills and mountains to gather medicines and other things. If those who seek the medicine roots, bark, and berries will ask me in a good way, if their thoughts are good, and their concern is for others, I will help them to find the medicines they seek. I shall know their thoughts. Also I am to help those who choose to meditate, pray, and fast in the bug-way-ji' (wild and natural places). I am the caretaker of all these places; the deep forests, swamps, mountains, and deep valleys. I am natural man. I am to be the different one, different in all ways. I shall not build a home or gather in o-day-nah-wing' (towns). Nor will I ever assemble with my own kind in tribes or nations. I will make no trails. Nor will I build ji-mon'-nug (canoes). I am to be alone in the quiet solitude and majesty of the natural world of the Creator. I shall know of man's presence, and I will know his thoughts. But only the Anishinabe shall know me. I am not to desire the companionship of Anishinabe or others . . . but only the Anishinabe shall know and honor me.

"Little brother, I have watched your journey and have known your thoughts. I will tell you of some but not all of the things you have wondered about. First, you must always treat the natural Creation with respect. When you **must** come through my territory, honor those places with Tobacco and good thoughts. Be not in fear. In that way you shall not become lost or confused and no harm will befall you. Be always in wonder and awe of all these natural works that you see; they are the hand and thought of the Creator, Gitchie Manito. These works, whether they be mountains, glaciers, waterfalls, the deepest swamps, or the wildest places, should never be changed, diverted, or disturbed. They are to remain as they are now just as I am to remain in my natural way."

Waynaboozhoo did not need to voice his thoughts as he visited with Bug-way'-ji-nini and they conversed through the night. Bug-way'-ji-nini continued to tell him many things that he had previously wondered about.

"Here upon the Earth is a plane . . . a place marked by time. Nowhere else in the Universe is time necessary. Remember that time belongs to the Creator and to none other. It is the one thing that is beyond the reach of man. None shall ever see it. Very few shall ever get to know it. Do not concern yourself with it. If you do, it will become an obsession and in the end you will be a slave to it.

"I know of many things that have puzzled you: the time you looked into the sky and wondered about the clouds, the time you felt rain drops on your face and looked into the distance to see rain falling in torrents, the time you felt warm and cold drafts of air sweep across your face, the time when you saw the heat dancing in waves over the plains.

"Here upon the lap of our Mother the Earth is a place and time that hangs between eight levels of elements. These elements are unseen but are as real and necessary for life as the water you drink. Of these eight elements, four are above the Earth and four are below the Earth. These elements are the things that must work together if life itself is to be. All these things working together lift the water into the clouds. Your oldest uncle Noo'-din (the wind) then blows this water to where it is needed. There it falls to the ground to nourish the grasses, flowers, and other beings who are dependent on it for life. Beyond this, there are elements that work together to change the seasons. The seasons are the evidence of time.

"Someday, when the time comes according to the Creator's plan, the cup of life will be measured by time. But even though time will be a part of life, life cannot exist without the other things we have spoken of. Remember, the cup of life is water and the cup is measured by time.

"If you should climb to the highest place, you will feel the absence of the air which is necessary to draw into your body in order to live. Likewise, if you would go into the Earth, soon it would get pitch black and there would be only poisons to breathe and draw into your body.

"As you walk on your journey, remember that there is a purpose to all things. There is a reason for the gentle rains and gentle winds as well as their opposites.

"Accept these things I give you. The evidence is all around you. See it, know it, accept it! Accept this knowledge as a 'Way of Knowing.' Accept it as you accept the knowledge of your own shadow. When your shadow is cast on the ground you are able to see it. But even though you do not see it at times, you know that your shadow is still there. Your shadow represents your relationship to Grandfather Sun and the Four Directions, and thus to the Universe.

"It is time for you to continue your journey. I will be with you, little brother, wherever your steps may take you. There is one last thing I wish to leave you and then we shall never talk again.

"You have a twin brother whom you have wondered about and whom you would seek. This I tell you: he is your other side in all things and in all ways. He is with you . . . do not seek him. Do not wish to know him, but understand him.

"You will walk the path of peace . . .
he would not.
You are kind . . . he is not.
You are humble . . . he is not.
You are generous . . . he is not.
You seek the good in things . . .
he does not.
You shall respect others . . . he will not.
You will seek the goodness in others . . .
he will not.
You are the light . . . he is the darkness.
Know that he is with you, understand him,
But do not seek him!"

With that, Bug-way'-ji-nini left Waynaboozhoo and vanished like a shadow into the woods.

Waynaboozhoo sat under the giant trees pondering all the things he had just received. His thoughts were interrupted by a hammering sound. It stopped and started again. It was Pa-pa-say' (the woodpecker). It said: "Someone is coming, expect someone, expect something. Someone is coming!"

Even today when Indian people hear the woodpecker's hammering they believe that this is an announcement of the approach of a visitor. Sometimes it is an announcement that thunder is coming.

The father of Waynaboozhoo sent Chi'-ani-mi-kee' (big thunder) and Chi-noo'-din (big wind) to meet his son. The trees started to sway uncontrollably. The fury of the wind and thunder in the giant trees made it seem like the whole world was going to come crashing down. Waynaboozhoo crouched under the giant trees for shelter. Big thunder shook the Earth. Wa-wa-sum' (lightning) bolts came and split some of the giant trees in half. Waynaboozhoo had never known such a terror in his whole life. He knew that the lightning he so feared was the mighty power of his father.

During the storm, Waynaboozhoo noticed that the thunder and lightning would break up and circle around spots on the Earth where a particular kind of rock lay exposed.

The big thunder, big wind, and lightning left and Waynaboozhoo sat trying to figure out the meaning of the special rocks. A bi-nay-shee′ (bird) overheard his thoughts and said to Waynaboozhoo, "This rock is called Ish-ko-day′-ah-sin′ (flint or fire rock). It has lightning and fire inside of it. The place where you find flint is a place of great power."

Waynaboozhoo placed Tobacco on one of the flint rocks.

Today when a storm approaches an Indian community, if someone puts Tobacco down in a respectful way, the storm will separate and go around the village.

Waynaboozhoo gathered a few pieces of the flint rock even though he did not know what he would do with them.

His father looked to the East from his seat in the West. He was surprised to see his son still under the giant trees. His son seemed to him a very beautiful and strong being. He was amazed and proud that his son had the strength and determination to travel so far just to see him. He knew that his son must have sacrificed many of his own desires in order to journey so far. But he was saddened because he knew that there was one last thing he had to do in order to fulfill the Creator's plan. He had to fight his son. He knew though, that in his conflict with his son that they would cause an end to all the conflict between fathers and sons yet to come on the Earth.

As Waynaboozhoo sat under the giant trees, he remembered what the buffalo had told him to do. He put Tobacco on the Earth and called to his father: "My father in the West, I have traveled far to see you. I have overcome many obstacles. Please show me your face, I wish to talk with you!"

Waynaboozhoo quickly reached into his bandolier bag and got out the special outfit that his Grandmother had made him long ago. He hurriedly dressed himself in the sacred clothes so that he would be fully prepared to meet his father.

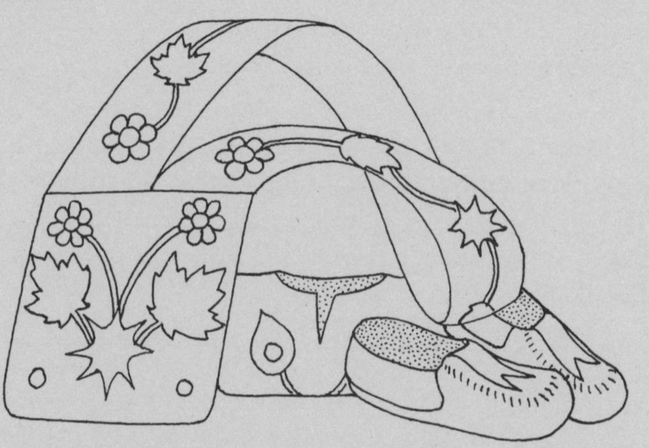

Waynaboozhoo waited patiently as the buffalo had instructed him to do. In four days his father appeared and spoke to him: "Ni-goos'-sis (my son), I know why you have come. My name is Mud-ji'-kee'-wis (a being with terrible power). I am the holder of the power of lightning and thunder!"

To Waynaboozhoo, his father seemed like a giant. His greatness was immense. His presence emanated a power. Waynaboozhoo sensed that his father was more of the Spirit World than he was of this world. He then understood that as a person, he was more of the physical world than of the world of his father. He understood, too, that in order to receive the answers to all his questions he must fight his father.

There are many descriptions of what followed. It is said that the fight between Waynaboozhoo and his father took them many places. Many people say that where they struggled, they overturned the Earth and laid everything flat as are the pa-pa-shkwag' (deserts) to this very day. The fight may have raged four days or four years. Time was lost during the struggle.

As they were fighting, Waynaboozhoo caught a glimpse of a pouch that hung by his father's side. It almost grabbed his interest but then his mind returned to the ensuing fight.

At last Waynaboozhoo felt that he could fight no more and that his father would overcome him. But at that moment, he remembered the flint that he had saved. With this piece of flint he reached out and slashed at his father.

His father stepped back in surprise.

Instantly, they both realized that each had such a power of his own that it would be wrong to destroy one another. In later days, Indian people remembered this and in their conflict with neighboring tribes they would never destroy an enemy. To destroy one part of the Creation would be to destroy it all.

His father spoke out: "My son you have surprised me! I admire you bravery and courage. I know you have many questions that have burned at your heart for a long time. I will answer all that you ask."

They talked for a long time. His father told him, "Your mother and I were together for many years. The love that we had was very powerful. When we had completed all the tasks asked of us by the Creator, we had to part and go our separate ways. I was given a place next to the western doorway to look to the East from whence life flows and see that all of history unfolds itself in a way that is pleasing to the Creator.

"Your mother was sent to the East to the doorway of motherhood and life-giving spring.

She lives there today with the Wa-bun'-ah-nung (Morning Star) and looks this way on the progress of the Earth's Creation. There are two stars that announce her coming before the dawn of each day. These stars have become like children to your mother. Your woman, the Firekeeper's Daughter, also cares for these children and is very close to your mother. She has not told you any of this because she realized that when the time was right all answers would be revealed to you.

"Between your mother in the East and myself in the West, all life from beginning to end is placed. My son, you are the connection between birth and death. All that you have experienced in your search for your Grandmother, for myself, and for your mother represents all of life to mortal man. It is a life that is full of responsibilities and tasks often at odds with personal desires, but a life that can also be full of happiness and fulfillment.

"You are half spirit and half man. The Creator has instructed me to send you to live among the people of the Earth, even as one of them. You are to be a guiding force to the men, women, and children that will follow you. You are to give them examples and teachings to make their lives happier and more meaningful. Give them examples of bravery, foolishness, humor, generosity. Give them examples of all things."

As his last act, Waynaboozhoo's father reached for the pouch that hung by his side. It was the pouch that Waynaboozhoo had noticed earlier in the fight. Now, he was captivated by its beauty. It was decorated with designs of lightning. Out of the pouch, Mud-ji'-kee'-wis pulled an O-pwa'-gun (Pipe) that was made of red stone and wrapped in Mush-ko-day-wushk' (Sage).

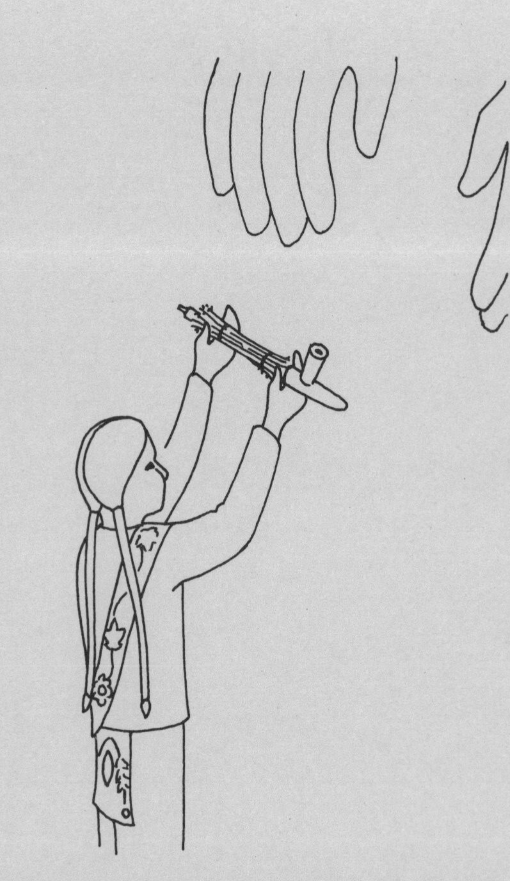

"My son, I want you to take this Pipe and keep it with you until the time comes when it is needed by the Earth's people. This Pipe is a symbol of peace and goodwill among all peoples and nations for all time. When you have finished your work on Earth, you will be given your eternal place and reward. After you have disappeared from the Earth, the Anishinabe will search for you by name and will honor you by clasping hands with each other and saying your name — 'Waynaboozhoo!' They will say this both when they come together and when they part. Your name shall be the greeting of new friends and relatives. Your name shall signify a brotherhood from which there is no good-bye or parting."

Waynaboozhoo was dumbfounded. He was honored with the gift of the Pipe. He was overwhelmed with his responsibility to his people in carrying the Pipe. He thought, too, of the lesson contained in his glimpsing the pouch at his father's side during the fight. It was almost as though it was a sign to him that we as human beings are often given glimpses of important parts of our future. Many times we do not perceive of the real importance of things that are revealed to us. They seem ordinary and insignificant to us. Waynaboozhoo resolved that he would pay closer attention to events in his life and thus come closer to understanding the plan of the Great Mystery.

Chapter 7

Waynaboozhoo and His Return to the People

Waynaboozhoo carefully put the O-pwa'-gun (Pipe) that his father had given him into the gah-skee'-bi-dag'-gun (bandolier bag) made many winters ago by his Grandmother. He looked at his father with admiration and respect. He felt love and respect return to him from his father's eyes.

"Father, on behalf of those who will come behind me, mi-gwetch for this Pipe. I will carry it well."

With that Waynaboozhoo turned to the East. He knew that the power of e-kan-da'-so-win' (knowledge) flowed from the East, but he understood that the paths of knowledge led in all directions. He began his journey back to his people with a single step. He walked with a feeling of fulfillment that he had never known before. He felt whole. He felt at one with the harmony of the Creation. He saw harmony in all that was around him — in the hills, in the streams, in the birds, and in the four-leggeds.

Waynaboozhoo found himself returning to familiar territory. He sensed that the forest of the giant trees lay just ahead. As he walked in the huge forests he knew that Bug-way'-ji-nini must be watching him. It was a reassuring feeling, indeed, that his oldest brother was always there.

Waynaboozhoo began to descend from the mountains. The prairies and plains ahead did not seem threatening to him anymore. Each step seemed to be a greeting to Mother Earth. He was proud of the tracks he was leaving behind him. They were moccasin tracks. He knew that the Creator, Gitchie Manito, would see his moccasin tracks just as he did the tracks of the Great Bear in the North. He sensed that the people of tomorrow would also see his tracks.

As he journeyed out onto the prairie, Noo'-din (the wind) began to blow into his face. A small whirlwind raced away just in front of him. His feet gave way to his desire to run. He found himself racing across the prairie trying to catch the whirlwind. The whirlwind was actually laughing at him. No matter how hard he ran the whirlwind could always stay in front of him. The whirlwind would dodge this way and that.

As they were racing across the prairie, the whirlwind called out to Waynaboozhoo: "My name is Bay-bee'-mi-say-si', catch me if you can! I am brother to the Gee-zhee-ba-sun' (tornado). I am brother to the waterspout of the oceans and seas. Their power is my power and my power is theirs. My brothers choose to destroy and, thus, demonstrate the awesome powers of the Creation. I love to tease instead. You can find me in all places and in all seasons. I think I love the swirling snow the best!"

Waynaboozhoo tried with all his might to catch the whirlwind!

Waynaboozhoo was annoyed at Bay-bee'-mi-say-si' and he shouted as he ran: "Tell me, brother, what purpose does your foolish life of teasing contribute to the Creation?"

Bay-bee'-mi-say-si' replied in a laughing voice: "My life may be foolish, Waynaboozhoo, but I have a purpose in life as noble as yours. My purpose is to tease those who take themselves too seriously. I tease the human beings, I tease the buffalo and all the four-leggeds, and I tease the spirits, too. There is a place for foolishness in the Creation. You better watch yourself or you will see me often. Remember:

There is a time to laugh,
a time to cry,
a time to live,
and a time to die."

Waynaboozhoo continued to question Bay-bee'-mi-say-si' as they ran across the prairie. "What are you, brother, spirit or wind?"

Bay-bee'-mi-say-si' replied: "I am wind . . . but I am spirit also. The Creator has placed spirits everywhere. There are spirits in the rocks. There are spirits in the water. All of us spirits are an extension of Gitchie Manito. All of us must answer to him. Greet us with Tobacco and we will tell you the secrets of the Creation."

Waynaboozhoo tried in vain to catch Bay-bee'-mi-say-si'. Just when he thought he had the whirlwind trapped against a rock, the dust would settle and Bay-bee'-mi-say-si' would be gone only to reappear at another spot! Finally Waynaboozhoo had to give up chasing Bay-bee'-mi-say-si'. The whirlwind disappeared in the distance. His laughter gradually mingled with the sound of the wind.

Waynaboozhoo had to rest for a while but soon he was again on his way to return to his people in the East. As he continued traveling, he thought of the words of Bay-bee'-mi-say-si'. He greeted the spirits that lived in the landscape here and there. He thought of blending foolishness and seriousness in his life. He thought of the power of the tornado, brother to the laughing Bay-bee'-mi-say-si'.

Waynaboozhoo now realized that life was truly a balance between joy and sorrow—times to be carefree and times to be careful. It was the purpose of Bay-bee'-mi-say-si' to provide that balance. It would be his spirit that would creep into ceremony and make a person laugh at the most serious moment. Even ceremonies can get too powerful and need the balance that Bay-bee'-mi-say-si' can provide. It would be Bay-bee'-mi-say-si' also who would step in and keep us from taking our search for fulfillment in life too seriously. If we try too hard to make the right decisions in life we might miss important signs that could lead us to the proper fork in life's path. Waynaboozhoo recognized that there was a fine line between joy and sorrow, laughter and crying. Mah-wee' (crying) could accompany joy as well as sorrow. Tears come with the highest form of joy. Just when sorrow seems overwhelming, Ba-pee-wug' (laughter) will come to provide the needed balance. Even at the death of a close friend, Bay-bee'-mi-say-si' comes to remind us of the good times we shared with our friend. He makes us laugh in the midst of sorrow. Bay-bee'-mi-say-si' is the bringer of laughter and the tears of joy.

The higher and rockier mountains that Waynaboozhoo crossed long before in his westward trip loomed up in the distance. He wondered if he would see Mi-sa'-be Mu-kwa' this time.

Just as he was pondering the power of the tornado, the Earth began to shake. Waynaboozhoo was alarmed because he had never felt this kind of sensation before. He reached for his Tobacco and placed some on the Earth. The Earth continued to shake. Waynaboozhoo thought to himself: "After all the things that I have done, what is it yet that I have not seen or done?" The Earth shook more and more and the fear in Waynaboozhoo grew. He remembered his encounter with Mi-sa'-be Mu-kwa' and what he had learned about fear. Waynaboozhoo pledged not to let wi-nan'-i-mi-zi-win' (terror) creep into his mind. He struggled to gain control over his fear and not to panic.

As Waynaboozhoo looked into the distance, he could hardly believe his eyes. A huge rocky mountain was slowly coming apart. Rocks tumbled this way and that as the shaking continued. Finally, it appeared as though the Earth opened up and swallowed the mountain. Nothing remained except the dust! The rumbling of the Earth gradually diminished. A strange quietness began to cover the land.

Waynaboozhoo thought over all he had seen. He knew that there must be lessons contained in the goos-koo-say' Ah-ki' (Earthquake). He realized that even the Earth, as generous and gentle as she is, could also be destructive. He thought of the words of Bug-way'-ji-nini about how the Creation should remain the same and how the natural world should never be "changed, diverted, or disturbed." He knew now that the power to change the Creation should lie only in the hands of Mother Earth and the Creator. Waynaboozhoo realized too that no matter how much he could experience and learn in life that there would always be more learning and new experiences ahead. He knew now that the road to knowledge is eternal.

Waynaboozhoo continued on his journey to the East full of wonder and awe at the power of the Creation that lay all around him—the wind, the Sun, the lightning, and the thunder.

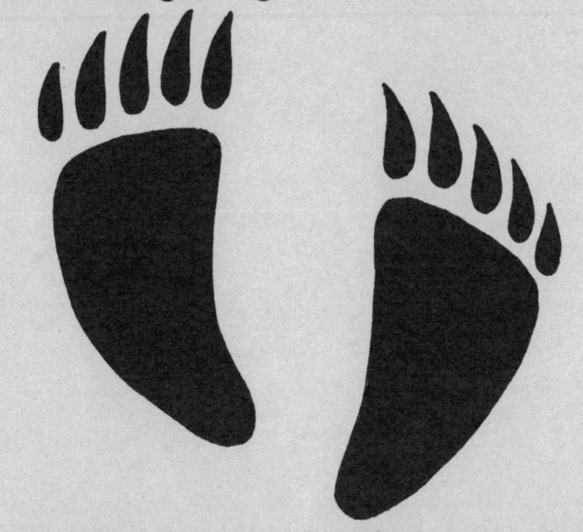

Waynaboozhoo crossed the mountains and put down Ah-say-mah' (Tobacco) as he crossed Mi-sa'-be Mu-kwa''s territory. As he traveled he began to recognize more and more of the land. He came to the banks of the O-gi-ma-kway'-zee-bee'. She was now swollen with torrents of water.

She, too, lived in a balance between peace and destruction. Waynaboozhoo thought to himself: "These must be the purifying waters of spring." He placed Tobacco in the swirling water and the Tobacco led him to a safe place to cross the river. Waynaboozhoo also gave his respects to the Michi-zee-bee' further ahead in the East. He came to the land of great lakes and forests that he knew to be the future home of the Anishinabe. With each step he sensed he was getting closer and closer to the settlements of his people.

One night as Waynaboozhoo made camp by a stream, he noticed Ay-si-bun' (a raccoon) sitting on the bank of the water. The raccoon was gathering clams from the sand near the stream's edge. The raccoon would open the shell of each clam and carefully wash the meat in the water. In this way Ay-si-bun' would clean his food before he ate it.

Waynaboozhoo watched the raccoon for a long time. When the raccoon had eaten his fill, he proceeded to wash himself all over. There seemed to be a lesson in the way Ay-si-bun' prepared his food and cleaned himself.

Waynaboozhoo realized that the raccoon was telling him that the body is special and sacred. We should be careful to put only clean things into our body because the body is what houses the spirit. The spirit is an extension of the Creator and the body is its Sacred Lodge. It is our responsibility, and ours alone, to keep our body clean and pure. In this way we can make a good home for our spirit.

Waynaboozhoo resolved that he would start taking better care of his body. After all, his body was really the only thing he possessed in the world. He knew that the Creator would notice if he made his body to be a clean and sacred place for his spirit. Waynaboozhoo pledged that from now on when he burned Tobacco and talked with the Creator, he would braid his hair and dress his body in his most special clothes. He knew the Creator could look through material things and see the true condition of his spirit, but he wanted to make a statement of pride about his body . . . the Sacred Lodge of his spirit.

As he rested in camp that night, Waynaboozhoo looked up into the sky and was overwhelmed at the beauty of the ah-nung-ug' (stars).

They seemed to stretch away forever into the Ish-pi-ming′ (Universe). He became lost in the vast expanse of stars. His Grandmother Nokomis had told him that all the stars represented the thoughts that the Creator sent out when he was looking for a place to put life. The knowledge of the Creator must be without end! If we were to seek that knowledge we would have to know every star. Waynaboozhoo sensed a pulse, a rhythm in the Universe of stars. He felt his own o-day′ (heart) beating within himself. The beat of his heart and the beat of the Universe were the same. Waynaboozhoo gazed into the stars with joy. He drifted off to sleep listening to his heart and comforted by the feeling of oneness with the rhythm of the Universe.

The next morning he awoke to the singing of birds. The birds were returning from their winter home in the South. They were returning with the seeds of life just as they did when the Earth was first created. They were reenacting their original instructions.

Waynaboozhoo looked around him and was surprised to see red berries growing here and there on the ground. He recognized them as the O-day′-min-nug′ (heart berries or strawberries) that Nokomis once told him about. It was said that they actually resembled the human heart in shape, structure and color. Just as the O-day′-min was connected to the strawberry plant by a vast system of leaves, runners, and roots, so was the heart connected to all the organs and parts of the human body. The heart was at the center of the human body. Nokomis had told him that O-day′-min was the last to bloom and the first to ripen of all the berries. The O-day′-min-nug′ became ripe just after the birds had returned from the South. Later, the Anishinabe would hold their spring ceremonies with the ripening of the O-day′-min-nug′. Nokomis had told him that the O-day′-min was a strong medicine plant. It could grow near the snow at the tops of the mountains as well as in the low valleys. The roots of the O-day′-min could be taken just before it became ripe and eaten to purify a person's blood. Waynaboozhoo realized that in order for the work of medicines to be complete, healing had to take place not only in a physical sense but in a spiritual sense as well. The body and mind had to be treated together because they represented the duality of all things. The O-day′-min was certainly evidence of this harmony that exists within the heartbeat of the Creation.

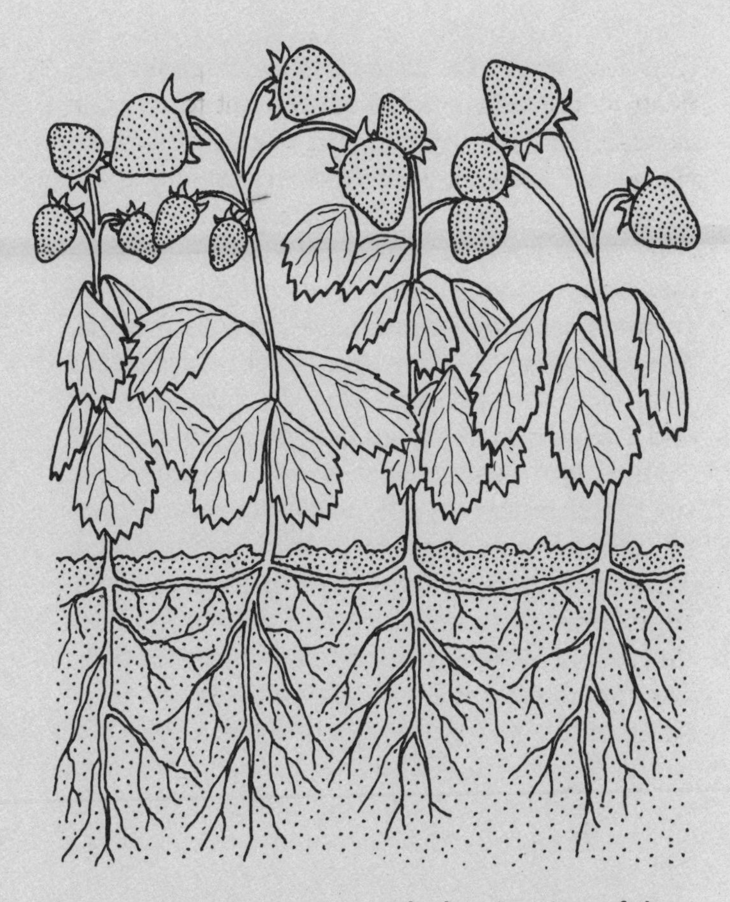

Waynaboozhoo put down Tobacco and ate a breakfast of strawberries. With the Sun rising into the sky in front of him, he continued on his journey. The Sun seemed to him to be the center of this part of the Universe. He sensed that the fire of the Sun was at the center of all things. He understood that this fire was at the na-way-ee′ (center) of his own body in a symbolic way and also in a real way. The fire of the Sun was at the heart of the most basic element of life. It was this fire that gave him life and kept him alive.

As Waynaboozhoo walked on he resolved to heed the advice of the whirlwind Bay-bee′-mi-say-si′. He would make his life among the Anishinabe to be a blend between wisdom and foolishness. He would make them laugh at his mistakes. Perhaps they could learn from his foolishness. But he would make them listen attentively to all the teachings that had been given to him. He remembered the Pipe in his bandolier bag and the instructions of his father. He knew that it was up to him to carry this Pipe with honor until it was needed by the Anishinabe.

His heart became lighter as he approached the land of the Anishinabe — the relatives of his four sons. He could see the smoke from their campfires curling up into the distant sky.

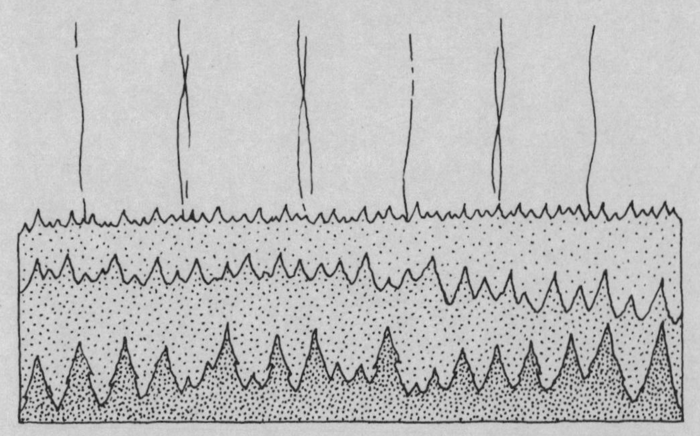

He remembered a na-ga-moon′ (song) his Grandmother used to sing when traveling and sounded his voice softly with those of the birds.

Waynaboozhoo began walking carefully through the land. It is true that he felt a special reverence for the Earth, but also he wanted his arrival in the land of his people to be a surprise.

Just then, Dee-deens′ (the bluejay) came to rest in a tree just ahead of Waynaboozhoo. Dee-deens′ started yelling as loud as he could. Waynaboozhoo pleaded with the bluejay to be quiet and even tried chasing him away, but Dee-deens′ only flew a little bit ahead yelling louder all the time. Waynaboozhoo sighed helplessly. If this kept up everybody throughout all the land would know he was coming!

Today, the Ojibway regard the bluejay as a gossip and tattletail. It is true that he offers an alarm when a stranger approaches, but it seems that Dee-deens′ gets a little carried away sometimes.

Human beings can also act like the bluejay. Usually in every village or town there is at least one person known as the town gossip. At times, the Ojibway jokingly refer to this person as Dee-deens.'

Just then, Waynaboozhoo was startled to hear a greeting called out from a short distance ahead. His presence was discovered. He was approached by a group of men. Their right hands were raised into the air with their palms forward in a gesture of friendship. Waynaboozhoo raised his hand to return the greeting. One of the men stepped forward and extended his right hand to Waynaboozhoo. Waynaboozhoo accepted the handshake and placed his left hand on his brother's shoulder. His brother, in turn, placed his own left hand on Waynaboozhoo's shoulder and greeted him with much joy. "Waynaboozhoo!" he said. Each of the men exchanged greetings with Waynaboozhoo in the same way. They said his name as they clasped his hand and shoulder. It was already just as his father had said it would be!

Waynaboozhoo felt a happiness, warmth, and fulfillment that he had never experienced before as he was led to join his people.

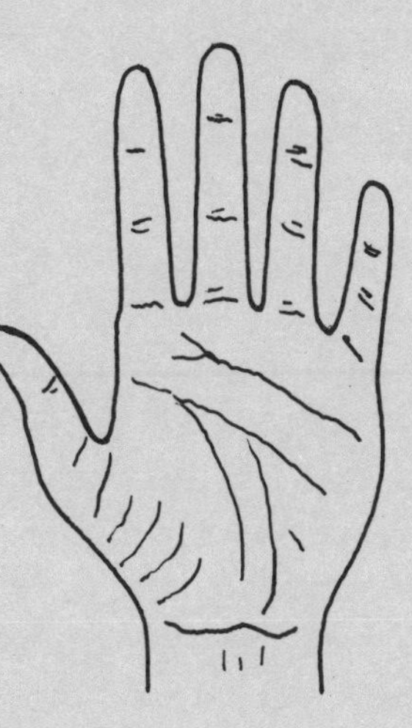

Chapter 8

"The Seven Grandfathers and the Little Boy"

The second people of the Earth grew in number and their villages began to spread across the land. But, in their early years, the second people had a very hard time. At first, they were a weak people. Diseases took many lives each year. There were many times when people would be killed by just stumbling and falling down. Waynaboozhoo did the best he could to help the Earth's people in their hard life, but it seemed that more help was needed.

Ojibway tradition tells us that there were Seven Grandfathers who were given the responsibility by the Creator to watch over the Earth's people. They were powerful spirits. The Seven Grandfathers recognized that life was not good for the people. They sent their Osh-ka-bay'-wis (helper) to the Earth to walk among the people and bring back to them a person who could be taught how to live in harmony with the Creation. Six times this spirit messenger went to Earth to try to find a person worthy enough to bring back to the Seven Grandfathers. Six times the spirit messenger failed. On his seventh journey, the Osh-ka-bay'-wis traveled to each of the four directions. The spirit came upon a village of people. He heard the people talking of a baby boy who had just been born to a young couple. The baby was still sucking on his mother's breast for food. The Osh-ka-bay'-wis suddenly realized that this baby was the one he should take to the Seven Grandfathers. He was innocent. His mind was untouched by corruption and pain of the world. This baby was still fresh from the Creator's side where he stayed before he came to his mother's womb. He had not yet opened his eyes and ears to the world.

The Osh-ka-bay'-wis found the baby asleep with his parents in a lodge on the outskirts of the village. The baby was in a hand-carved dik-ki-na'-gun (cradle-board) wrapped in fine animal skins that were decorated with quills from Gawg (the porcupine). His parents and his people must have thought a lot of him. The Osh-ka-bay'-wis left a pouch of Tobacco and a piece of the child's clothing behind to show the people that the baby did not fall victim to some wild animal.

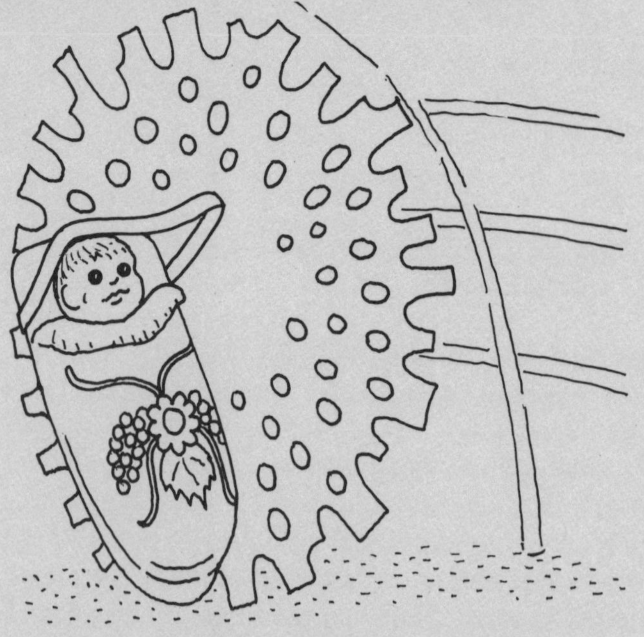

The Osh-ka-bay'-wis took the baby boy back to the lodge of the Seven Grandfathers. The Seven Grandfathers looked on the sleeping baby. "He is too weak," one said. "He could not stand

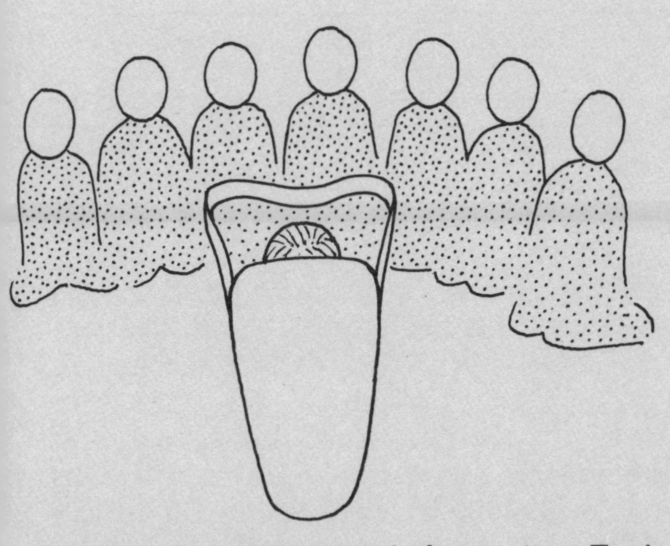

the sight of us or the sound of our voices. To do so would be fatal to him." One of the Grandfathers instructed the Osh-ka-bay'-wis, "Take this boy and show him all of the Creation, show him the Four Quarters of the Universe."

The Osh-ka-bay'-wis took the boy and did as he was instructed. It took a long time to travel so far and teach the boy so much. They traveled completely through all of the A-nung'-go-kwan' (Star World).

Herein lies a lesson for us today. We must begin very early with our children in instructing them in these teachings. Children are born with fully-developed senses and are aware of what is happening around them. They can even communicate with the Spirit World. Most of us as human beings are so far removed from the Spirit World that we cannot tell what an infant is saying. Let us learn from the Seven Grandfathers the importance of giving our young children the teachings they will need to guide them in their later lives.

The boy was seven years old when they returned to the lodge of the Seven Grandfathers. The Grandfathers saw them coming and realized that the boy had grown to be strong with a mind that was sharp and curious about everything around him.

As the boy approached the Grandfather's lodge he felt a power stronger than anything he had ever felt before. He looked up at the Osh-ka-bay'-wis and realized that this was his zhi-shay' (uncle)—someone who had taught him how to survive in the world. He realized that his uncle was a son of the Creator. He understood that he, too, was from the Creator's side as are all people.

As the boy came closer to the lodge a strong fear overcame him. The closer they came, the stronger his fear grew. His uncle, the Osh-ka-bay'-wis, comforted him. As they approached the door of the lodge a voice rang out: "Have you brought the boy?"

"Yes," the uncle answered. "I have him with me and he is ready to come inside."

With that the door of the lodge was opened and inside sat the Seven Grandfathers. "Be-in-di-gain'" (Come in), they said to the boy and his uncle, the Osh-ka-bay'-wis. As the boy stepped inside he noticed that the door of the lodge was facing the Sun in the West and that the Seven Grandfathers sat in the East—the place his uncle told him was the source of all knowledge. The Seven Grandfathers were dressed in very beautiful clothes and their hair was as white as snow. On their faces was a glow of peace and happiness.

The Grandfathers talked to the boy in a way that seemed as though they were not talking at all but using their minds to just think the words. The Grandfathers told the boy of how he was taken from his mother and father and how his parents were expecting him to return some day.

Each of the Seven Grandfathers took a gift out of the vessel and gave it to the boy.

The first Grandfather pointed to an aw-kik' (vessel) that was covered with a cloth made of four different colors. Each color stood for one of the Four Directions. The Grandfather said, "Of these colors, mis-skwa' (red) stands for the South. Muk-a-day' (black) stands for the West. Wa-bish-ka' (white) stands for the North. And o-za-wahn' (yellow) stands for the East. These colors represent the four races of man that the Creator placed on the Earth.

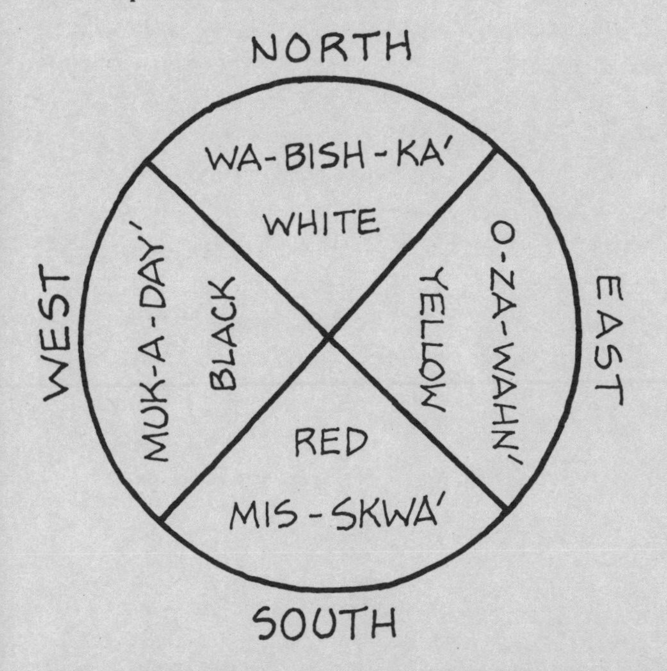

The Grandfather pulled the cloth aside and instructed the boy to look inside the vessel. It was a very quick glimpse, but inside the boy saw beauty that he could not understand. He saw colors that had never been seen before. He felt a peace that he had never known before. He saw all of yesterday and all of tomorrow. The vessel was like an opening and out of it came a music such as the boy had never heard. All that could possibly be imagined flashed before the boy's eyes in just a short moment.

The first Grandfather reached into the vessel and brought out a substance on his hand. He then reached over and rubbed this substance on the boy. "I give you this gift!" he said. Then he passed the vessel to the next Grandfather who also reached inside and rubbed a new and beautiful gift on the boy. The vessel was passed to each of the Grandfathers just as the Waterdrum is passed from one person to another in our ceremonies today. Each of the Grandfathers gave the boy a gift.

When they had finished the Grandfathers instructed the Osh-ka-bay'-wis to find someone to return with the boy to his people. Four times the Osh-ka-bay'-wis searched the Earth without finding anyone. On his fifth try, the Osh-ka-bay'-wis came upon Ni-gig' (an otter) playing on the bank of a creek. But the otter would not listen to him. He was too busy playing. The Osh-ka-bay'-wis returned again to Ni-gig' and told him of the task that he was needed for, but the otter just yawned and continued playing. On his seventh try the Osh-ka-bay'-wis convinced the otter to return with him and they journeyed to the lodge of the Seven Grandfathers.

The otter received his instructions from the Seven Grandfathers and paid attention to each detail. Finally, the otter and boy set off on their long journey. The boy had been given a huge bundle to take to his people from the Seven Grandfathers. Ni-gig′ and the boy took turns carrying the bundle. Along the way, they stopped seven times. At each stop a spirit came and told the boy the meaning of one of the seven gifts that were given to him out of the vessel of the Grandfathers.

(1) To cherish knowledge is to know **WISDOM**.
(2) To know **LOVE** is to know peace.
(3) To honor all of the Creation is to have **RESPECT**.
(4) **BRAVERY** is to face the foe with integrity.
(5) **HONESTY** in facing a situation is to be brave.
(6) **HUMILITY** is to know yourself as a sacred part of the Creation.
(7) **TRUTH** is to know all of these things.

The spirits taught the boy that for each gift there was an opposite, as evil is the opposite of good. He would have to be careful to instruct his people in the right way to use each gift.

Also at each stop, the boy found a strange kind of small shell sprinkled here and there on the ground. He sensed something special about these shells. He put down Tobacco and took a few of them at each stop.

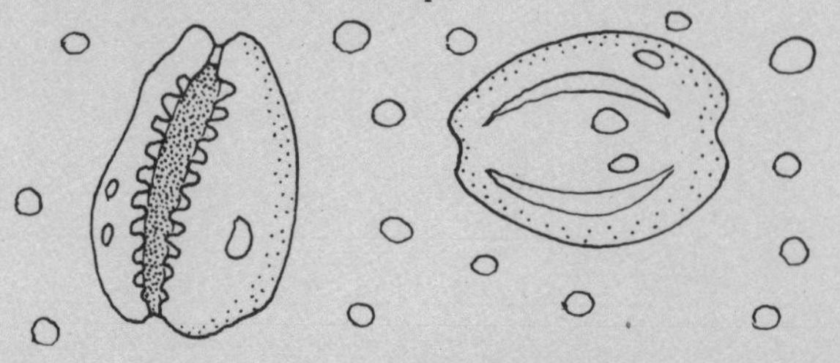

For four days the boy and the otter stopped at each place. But in the Spirit World, time cannot be compared to our time on Earth. The stops could have lasted even four years of time on Earth.

During this time the boy grew into manhood. He and the otter somehow realized that the next time they would set their burden down, they would be in the land of his people. At last they came upon a large body of water. They could see the people on the other shore. They looked poor and hungry. The otter realized that these people did not have the true Wayn-dah-ni-muk′ no-di-noon′ (Four Directions) and therefore, could not live in harmony with the power that each direction offers. The otter dived into the water and swam to the middle of the lake. There he shouted to the people and told them that he would show them the true Four Directions so that they could live in harmony. The people cheered and watched

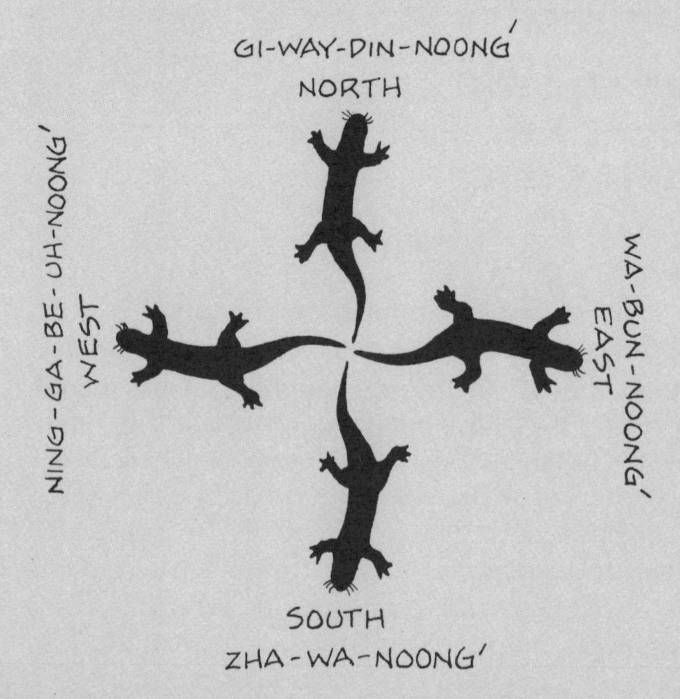

the otter as he swam to the East and then back to the middle of the lake. He then swam to the South and back to the middle. The otter did this with each of the Four Directions.

The otter finally returned to get his friend who was getting to be an old man by all the time he had seen in the Spirit World. He escorted the old man to his people. The old man carried a huge, heavy bundle. It was a great power that he was to share with his people. The otter showed the man the way. Then the otter realized that he had finished the task that the Seven Grandfathers had asked of him. He said to the old man, "My friend, we have been many places together. We have overcome all obstacles." At this time the otter produced one of the strange shells that were at each of the stopping places and held it out to the old man.

"These are very special shells. They are an important gift and will figure into your life at a later time. They represent the shell that the Creator used to blow his breath on the four sacred elements and give life to Original Man. Keep this shell with you always. It is called the Megis Shell.

"I have now done what the Grandfathers asked of me. I will continue to serve you if you can follow me!"

At this, the otter remembered all the playful moments of his past and ran straight up a tall tree and sat in the top laughing at his friend holding the heavy bundle down below. The otter is the one today who accompanies the new-comers into the Midewiwin Lodge. He accompanies them only through their first degree. Then they must part.

Realizing that he must now leave his brother the otter, the old man picked up his bundle and

continued to make his way toward the village. On the outskirts of the village the old man came upon a very old couple. This couple somehow knew that this man with the heavy bundle was their son even though his hair was white like theirs. The only thing that had kept them alive was the memory of their son and the faith that he would come back.

The old man pulled a gift out of his bundle and said to his parents, "I give you this. It represents the power, love, and mercy of the Creator." He continued on to visit and talk with the rest of his people. To the middle of the village he went with his bundle and all the people followed. At the village's center he stopped and put down his bundle.

With all the people gathered round, the old man told them of his journey to the lodge of the Seven Grandfathers. He gave the people the seven gifts that the Grandfathers had given him out of the vessel. He told the people of the dangers that came with each gift. He gave them the understanding of opposites.

He told them of the way the Grandfathers said to live in order to have a strong physical body. He told them that the nee-zho-day′ (twin) of physical existence was spiritual existence. In order for the people to be completely healthy they must seek to develop themselves spiritually and find a balance between the physical and the spiritual worlds. The old man gave the people the avenue to use for this spiritual development. He gave them the Ba-wa-ji-gay′-win (Vision Quest). He gave others the capability to seek out the knowledge of the Spirit World through fasting, dreaming, and meditation.

With the old man's return, the people became better adjusted physically to live on Earth. The people had a sense of hope that gave them the strength to face life's daily tasks. No longer did accidents and diseases claim so many lives. With the knowledge of the Four Sacred Directions that the otter gave them and with the gradual use of herbal medicines to treat illnesses, the people approached that delicate balance that lies in living in harmony with all of the Creation.

It only remained now the for people to follow the me-ka-naynz′ (path) laid out before them by the old man for the development of the spiritual side of life.

Chapter 9

The Old Man and the First Midewiwin Ceremony

In our last chapter, we learned of how the little boy was taken from the lodge of his parents and taken by the Osh-ka-bay′-wis to the lodge of the Seven Grandfathers. There he was given seven gifts and many teachings. By the time the little boy returned to his people he was an old man. He gave physical stability to his people. He also gave them the ability to seek spiritual development through fasting and Ba-wa-ji-gay′-win (the Vision Quest). We now join the same old man in his village.

After a period of time, a young boy in the village became like an Osh-ka-bay′-wis to the old man. Somehow the two were drawn together. The young boy began to work for the old man. In exchange, the old man gave stories to the boy about his experiences with the Seven Grandfathers. The young boy absorbed everything.

For some strange reason, the young boy became very ill. Many felt that his death was certain.

The old man gathered the women of the village and instructed them that they, as women, symbolized the life-giving force of the Earth. Because of this, he wanted them to build a lodge in which he could perform a ceremony to ask that the young boy be given continued life.

This was to be the origin of the Midewiwin Lodge.

While the old man remembered everything he had experienced with the Seven Grandfathers, he still had no ritual to guide him.

The next day before dawn, the women set out to gather materials to make the lodge for the old man. They gathered Ini-na-tig′ (maple) saplings because they knew that the maple was a life-giving being. They used the maple saplings for the frame of the lodge. With the guidance of the old man, they constructed the first Midewiwin Lodge.

The lodge was built in line with the path of the Sun. It had an eastern doorway and a western doorway. The top was left open. Along the sides they put balsam, spruce and fern to further draw

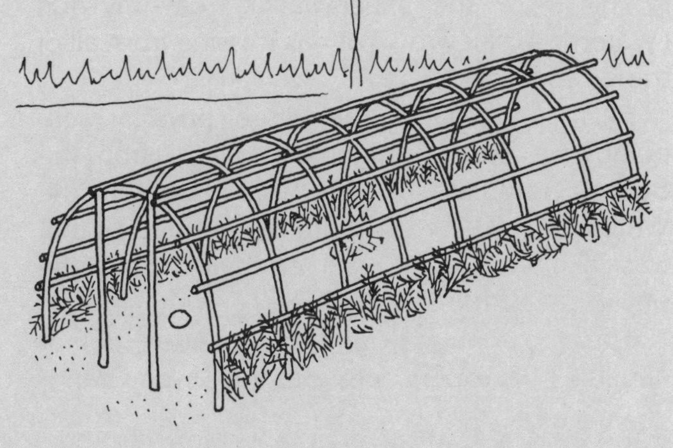

upon the nourishment of the plant world. They placed water inside the doorway of the lodge.

These preparations took two days.

On the morning of the third day, the old man announced that on daybreak of the next day, the ceremony would begin and that the young boy should be prepared that night.

The old man knew that some essential part of the lodge was missing. He tried to relive the time that he was with the Seven Grandfathers to see if there was some part of the instructions that he had missed. He meditated all day to try to discover the missing part of the ceremony. When the Sun was sinking in the West at the finish of the day, the old man turned from watching the sunset and looked to the East. He saw in the eastern sky what looked like a huge tree. The tree appeared to be coming closer. The old man thought, "This must be what is missing!" As he watched, the tree changed into the very same vessel that the Seven Grandfathers had in front of them when he had visited their lodge in his childhood. He remembered that the Grandfathers had reached into the vessel and had taken something out with their hands. They then touched the different parts of his body with these substances.

This was the Mi-tig-wa-kik' day-way'-gun (Waterdrum)! It was what was missing from all of the arrangements!

He realized that all the gifts of physical well-being that he had brought to the people from the Seven Grandfathers were symbolized in the Waterdrum. The Waterdrum represented all that was necessary for life. It embodied both the physical and the spiritual.

The old man was able to remember other details of his experiences with the Seven Grandfathers. He was able to put everything in order. He knew that more knowledge would come to him with the coming of the morning Sun.

Before daybreak the next day, the old man arose and built a small ish-ko-day' (fire). Into this fire he placed his Tobacco offerings. At that time his uncertainty about the coming ceremony was washed away. He was filled with inspiration. Some people say that this was the first Morning Ceremony.

He saw the Wa-bun' ah-nung' (Morning Star) in the East. He recognized this star to be the Mother of the First Mother—the Mother from which came the mother of Original Man, Waynaboozhoo. He realized that the lodge fire of the mother of Waynaboozhoo now marked the place of Wa-bun' ah-nung'. He saw that there were two stars that came before Wa-bun' ah-nung' that announced her coming. He knew these to be her children.

The Sun came gradually after the Morning Star and clarified the teaching to the old man that woman always comes first. She precedes man. She precedes Grandfather Sun. Woman lights the way for man just as Grandmother Moon lights the way for the night world.

During this Morning Ceremony the old man was given the remaining instructions that he needed to conduct the first Midewiwin ritual. From the eastern doorway the knowledge flowed to him of what to do. He was given the knowledge of how to construct the Waterdrum and what her different parts symbolized. The first Waterdrum was constructed at Sunrise of that fourth day. Even today, it takes four days to prepare for the Midewiwin ceremony.

Just at sunset on the third day of preparations,
the old man received a vision in the eastern sky.

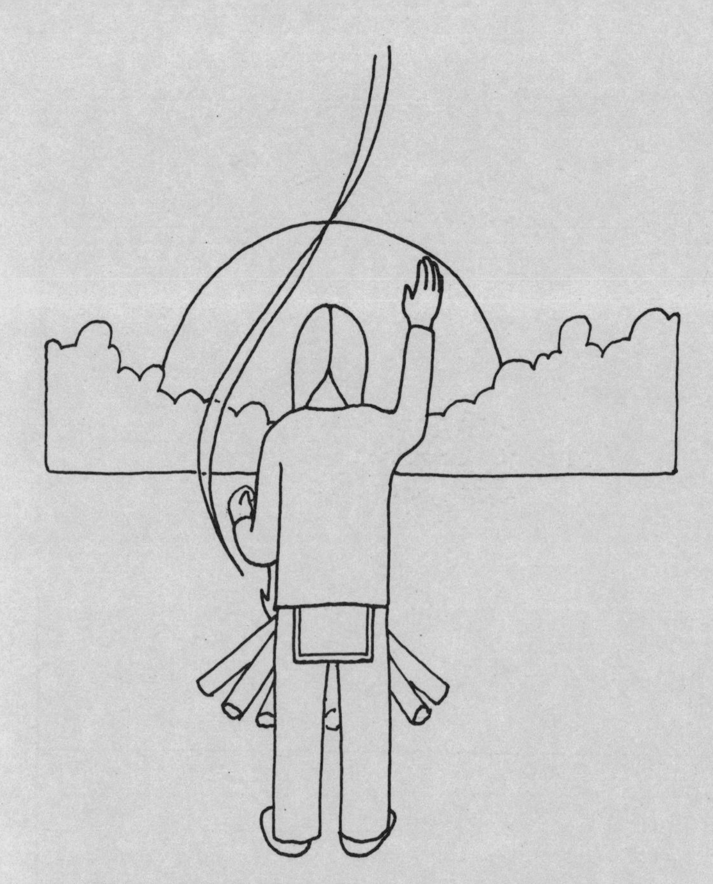

He made the Waterdrum to resemble in every way the vessel that sat in front of the Seven Grandfathers.

He made the body of the Waterdrum out of a hollowed-out log. The wooden body of the drum is symbolic of all of our plant brothers and sisters with whom we must learn to live in a respectful way.

The head of the Waterdrum was made of deerhide. It represents and honors all of our four-legged brothers and sisters. The deerhide brings with it the qualities and gifts of the Wa-wa-shkesh'-she (deer). It gives the sound of the drum a soft but high-pitched quality. It gives speed and agility to the drumbeat. It gives a quality of peace and gentleness to the Waterdrum.

Before he placed the head on the Waterdrum, the old man partially filled the wooden shell of the drum with water. This ni-bi' (water) is said to represent the life blood of Mother Earth, the blood that flows through her, carries food to her, and purifies her. This water represents the life-giving force of Mother Earth that purifies and gives life to our bodies as well.

Into the water the old man sprinkled a little Ah-say-ma' to remember how Tobacco was given to us so that we might talk with the Creator.

The old man attached the head to the Waterdrum with a hoop that was carefully fitted over the top of the drum. This hoop represents the Sacred Circle in which all natural things move. It represents the seasons of the Earth. It represents the birth, growth, and death of all living things. It represents the movement of the waters on Mother Earth. It represents the sacred bond between man and woman.

Sometime in later days, the Anishinabe attached the head to the Waterdrum by tying seven small, round stones into the deerhide head. These stones represent and give honor to our Mother the Earth. They also represent the Seven Original Teachings that came to the Ojibway. It is said that these stones can only be found today in places where the Waterdrum has sounded her voice in the past.

When the seven stones are used, the head is fastened to the Waterdrum by tying the stones to the deerhide head and then to the base of the drum. There are seven different ways used to tie the Waterdrum. Each way represents a sacred teaching. The tie that is used on the Waterdrum for a certain ceremony is determined only after meditation by the Osh-ka-bay'-wis. Today, the young apprentices gather around to watch, not only to learn the different ties, but to listen to the teachings that are often told while the drum is being tied. It is said that much can be learned about the ceremony that is to follow by paying attention to how the drum ties. The Waterdrum, in this way, is said to speak to those who handle her in a respectful way.

The old man adjusted the hoop so that the deerhide was pulled tight over the wooden shell. He took great care to straighten the deerhide that hung down below the hoop. He understood this to be the wee-nes'-si-see' (hair) of the drum, hair that should be well-kept and free of tangles.

After the Waterdrum was tied, the old man pulled a plug out of a hole in the wooden shell. He held the drum up to the Creator and blew his breath into the drum. This he did to represent the life-giving breath of the Creator, that breath to which all life is ultimately linked.

The old man carved a day-way'-ga-na-tig' (drumbeater) out of a living root that he took from the Earth. He carved the head of the drumbeater with a curve to represent the neck of the crane and the loon. These birds would later come into importance in the life structure of the Anishinabe.

When all these preparations had been done, the old man took the Waterdrum and sounded its voice four times. The sound of the Waterdrum

was carried by the wind to all directions. This was done to announce to the village that the long-awaited ceremony was about to begin. The people began to come from everywhere to witness this first Midewiwin ceremony and give the support of their prayers to the sick young boy who had now been placed in the lodge.

All at once the old man remembered the teachings about the Megis Shell that he had received from the otter. It was the shell that the Creator used in blowing his breath into the four sacred elements when he created Original Man. His mind went back to the time long ago when he picked up the Megis Shells at the seven stopping places on his journey home from the lodge of the Seven Grandfathers. He reached into a leather pouch that hung by his side and retrieved one of these shells. He placed the shell at the doorway of the lodge. This Megis Shell has since become an integral part of the Midewiwin religion.

The old man took the drumbeater and sounded the Waterdrum again four times. The ceremony was beginning. The lodge was full of the village people. Those who could not fit in the lodge gathered by the sides of the lodge and gave their support from the outside. The ceremony lasted most of the day. By sundown, strength had miraculously returned to the sick boy who lay in the lodge.

The boy recovered completely from his illness and in the days to come received all the teachings about the Midewiwin ceremony from the old man. He grew into manhood. When the old man finally passed away, the young man carried on the Midewiwin ceremonies and teachings. He chose four assistants to teach the sacred ways he had learned so the Midewiwin would be alive to guide the future generations of the Anishinabe.

This teaching of the first Midewiwin ceremony and how the boy was cured of his sickness establishes the order for the priesthood of the Midewiwin. It established the relationship that should exist between elders and youth among all people. This relationship provides a link between the knowledge that must flow between generations. It provides the links for an unbroken string of lives all the way back to our origin as a people.

As the Midewiwin developed, it gave the people new meaning to their lives. It became a strong and guiding force. Men, women and children were inspired by it.

The first ceremony that the old man conducted represented the first degree of the Midewiwin. As time passed and the structure of the people developed, there came the second, third, and fourth degrees. With each degree came another set of knowledge that built upon the original first degree. Each degree was like an elevation in which more of the knowledge and power of the Midewiwin was revealed.

As the people grew in the Midewiwin Way they began to use the gift that the old man had left to them. They began to fast in order to seek visions. The vision represented a quest for knowledge and guiding principles in life.

There came through the Waterdrum songs of prayer, beauty and thanksgiving. As the Midewiwin developed so did the people develop both physically and spiritually. The music of the people grew. The teachings grew. This "Beauty Way" of speaking and walking reinforced all the teachings of generosity, love, respect, honor, humility, obedience, and hope. Life became a song and prayer again.

As time went on the Waterdrum took on different responsibilities. Different designs and colors came to represent the various degrees and responsibilities that were given to the Waterdrum.

The otter came to represent the first degree. Other animals came forth to represent the body of knowledge that came with each succeeding degree. It took many years, perhaps centuries, for the eight known degrees of the Midewiwin Lodge to develop. All through the years and to this day there are very few who ever reach the eighth degree.

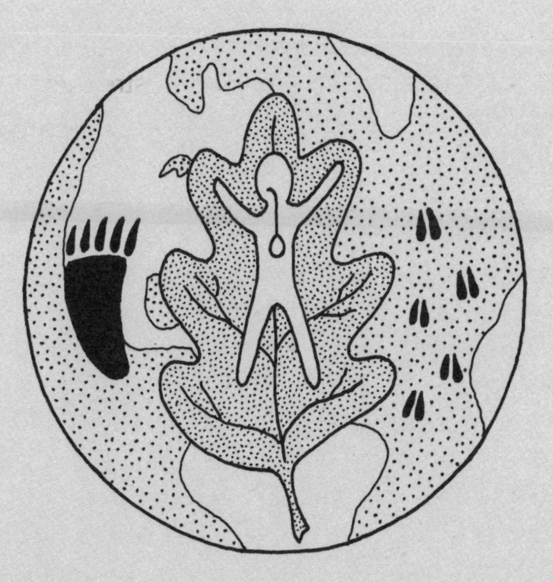

The Midewiwin Lodge helped to develop this humility in the people. The people were given a gift of unlimited development. But this development had its dangers . . . its twin. The people could help themselves but they could also destroy themselves.

It is important for us to remind ourselves of our place in the Universe. We are but a small part.

Through these ways the people were able to develop a rapport with all the other beings of the Earth who shared the same space and time. They were able to communicate with all the other things of the Ish-pi-ming′ (Universe). They understood that they belonged to the Four Levels of the Earth: the Mother Earth, the plant life, the animal life, and the human beings. In this chain, the human beings were the last to come. It was understood that human life could not survive without any of the preceding levels, while the other levels could survive very easily without the human beings.

Chapter 10

The Clan System

In our last chapter we learned how the first Midewiwin ceremony came into being. We learned how the Waterdrum came to the people. The Midewiwin religion taught the people how to use the powers of the Spirit World to treat their sicknesses. The Midewiwin gave the people a sense of spiritual strength to be balanced with its twin — the physical side of life. The people were no longer frail and began to live longer.

But the Creator remembered how the Earth's people had suffered in the past. He decided that the Earth's second people needed a system — a framework of government to give them strength and order. To do this he gave them the O-do-i-daym-i-wan′ (Clan System).

There were seven original o-do-i-daym′-i-wug′ (clans):

Ah-ji-jawk′ (Crane)

Mahng (Loon)

Gi-goon′ (Fish)

Mu-kwa′ (Bear)

Wa-bi-zha-shi′ (Martin)

Wa-wa-shesh′-she (Deer)

Be-nays′ (Bird)

Each of these clans was given a function to serve for the people.

The Crane and the Loon Clans were given the power of chieftanship. They were given the people with natural qualities and abilities for leadership. Each of these two clans claim to be the original Chief Clan. They were both given the respect of chieftanship. By working together the Crane Clan and the Loon Clan gave the people a balanced government with each serving as a check on the other.

Between the two Chief Clans stood the Fish Clan. It was sometimes referred to as the Water Clan. The Fish Clan was made up of the intellectuals of the people. They were sometimes called "star gazers," since they were known for their constant pursuit of meditation and philosophy. The Fish Clan members would settle disputes between the two Chief Clans if a deciding vote needed to be cast. This built-in ability of the Clan System to resolve differences of opinion greatly added to its effectiveness as a governing body.

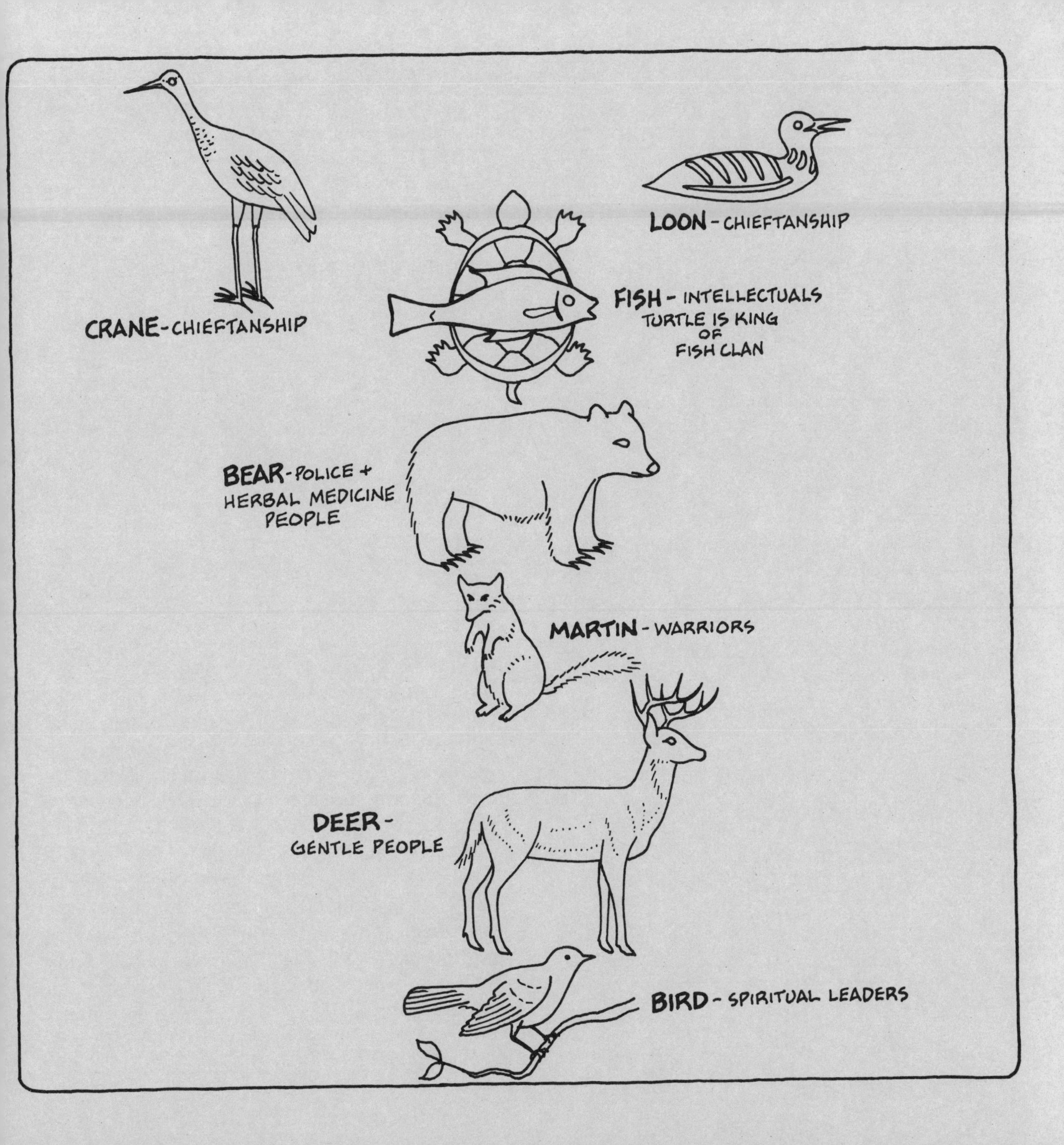

CRANE-CHIEFTANSHIP
LOON - CHIEFTANSHIP
FISH - INTELLECTUALS
TURTLE IS KING
OF
FISH CLAN
BEAR-POLICE +
HERBAL MEDICINE
PEOPLE
MARTIN - WARRIORS
DEER-
GENTLE PEOPLE
BIRD - SPIRITUAL LEADERS

The Bear Clan served as the police force of the people. They spent most of their time patrolling the outskirts of the village so as to ward off any unwelcome visitors. Because of the large amount of time they spent close to nature, the Bear Clan became known for their knowledge of plants whose roots, bark, or leaves could be used as medicines to treat the ailments of their people.

The Martin Clan served as the warrior clan for the people. They provided the force to protect the village at all costs from outside invaders. They became known as master strategists in planning the defense of their people.

The Deer Clan was known as the clan of gentle people. They were the pacifists. It was said that the people of the Deer Clan would not even indulge in using harsh words of any kind. They were the poets of the people.

There are those who say that it was the moose and not the deer who was the leader of this clan. Others in the northern regions of this hemisphere claim that it was the carribou who was the clan head. Eventually all the clans diffused out into different divisions, but always one animal represented the head or king of the clan. The turtle, for instance, was the head of the Fish Clan.

The Bird Clan was the final clan and represented the spiritual leaders of the people. Its members were noted for their intuition and sense of knowledge of what the future would bring. They were said to have the characteristics of the eagle, the head of their clan, in that they pursued the higher elevations of the mind just as the eagle pursued the higher elevations of the sky.

So the Creator gave the people the seven original clans to provide leadership in all areas. One of the natural laws that the Creator gave the people along with the Clan System was that there was to be no intermarriage of people in the same clan. In this way the blood of the Earth's second people would be kept pure and strong.

It is said that the people of the Deer Clan once violated this natural law and began marrying within their clan. The Deer Clan people were sent warnings. Their children started to be born with defects and abnormalities. They made no correction in their ways. Finally, the Creator was so disturbed by this departure from the way of harmony that he destroyed the Deer Clan in its entirity. For this reason there are no members of the Deer Clan among the Ojibway people today.

The Clan System became an important part of the Midewiwin Lodge. Each of the clans was given a function and place in the Midewiwin. All the clans were held together by the force of the Waterdrum.

It was the responsibility of the Bear Clan to guard the doorway of the Midewiwin Lodge. Inside the lodge, the clans would take their positions in the order that was given to them by the Creator:

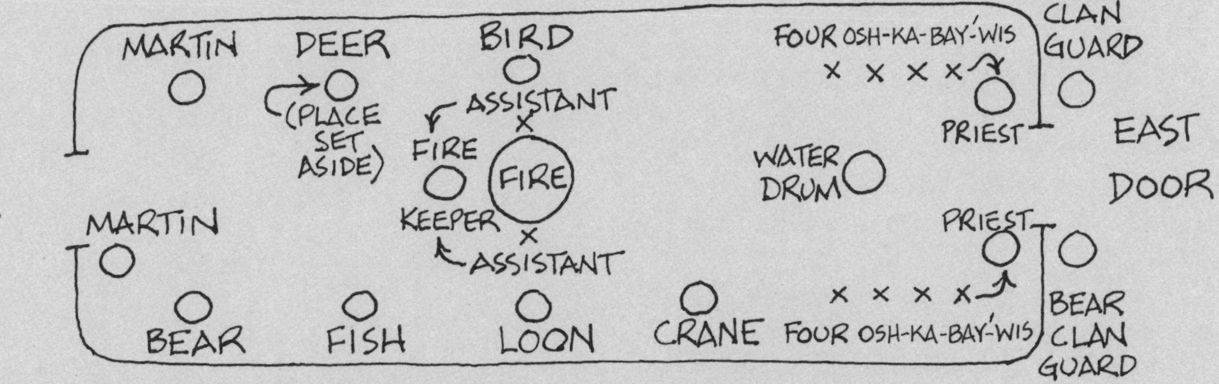

After the Clan System was given to the people, the Seven Grandfathers sent seven spiritual beings to Earth to clarify how the Clan System was to be used and to amplify the meaning of many gifts often taken for granted in life. The beings came to the people out of the water. They brought many teachings meant to sharpen the senses of the people. It is said that the first five beings brought messages pertaining to the five senses of man: touch, smell, taste, hearing, and sight. The sixth being brought teachings about ah-mun′-ni-soo-win′ (intuition)—a special sense that goes beyond the ordinary senses. It was a special sense that few people recognize in their lives.

When the people looked to the seventh being to see what gift it was that he brought to them, they saw that his eyes were covered by a blind.

The people asked the seventh being, "Why do you hide your eyes from us! What have you brought us?"

The being answered, "What I have to give, you may not be ready for!"

The people insisted that the seventh being uncover his eyes. When he lifted the blind from his face there were shrieks and screams from the people. All those who saw his eyes fell over dead.

The seventh being turned and walked back into the water but he shouted to the people that he would return when the proper time came, if it ever came.

Many people have speculated as to what gift it was that the seventh being brought. Most agree that it was the ability to see into the future (nee-goni-wa′-bun-gi-gay-win′). The people may yet see the seventh being return with this gift for everybody if the time is made right.

While the Clan System was in power, the Ojibway suffered no famine, sickness, or epidemics. There was said to be no wars and very little violence in these days when the Clan System was strong. In the Clan System was built equal justice,. voice, law and order. It reinforced by its very nature the teachings and principles of a sacred way of life.

It is interesting to think of where our society might be today if the people had held the Clan System together in its original form and power.

Chapter 11

"The Pipe and the Eagle"

In the preceding two chapters, we learned how first the Midewiwin and then the Clan System came to the people and gave them strength and stability. The Midewiwin provided the people with the spiritual strength that they needed to couple with their physical well-being to become whole and balanced within the Creation. The Clan System gave the people a stable and well-functioning social and governing system.

There followed a long period of peace and prosperity for the people. The Waterdrum brought many songs to the people. Cultural ways blossomed. Life was full.

However, in time, conflict and warfare began to appear again on the Earth. Conflict became so prevalent that almost all of the people's time was consumed in the preparations for war and in the making of war. Even the ceremonies became oriented to conflict so that a tribe or band might gain spiritual guidance or favor that they could use to gain more territory. More and more of the religious teachings were twisted to apply to conflict instead of the life-giving ways of the Waterdrum and the original Midewiwin. Factions began to emerge within the tribes out of which warrior societies developed. Elitism became the example for young people to follow instead of peace, humility and generosity. Face painting grew as a practice among the people as pride overcame humility. Soon there were too few gi-wi-say'-i-nini-wug' (hunters) left to provide for the families. The best hunters became the proud and vain warriors.

At this time, the spirit of Waynaboozhoo emerged among the people. He bore the O-pwa'-gun (Pipe) wrapped in Sage that was given to him by his father many years before. Waynaboozhoo showed the people how to smoke tobacco in the Pipe and in so doing seal peace, brotherhood and sisterhood among the bands, tribes and nations. Waynaboozhoo told the people that the smoke that came from the Pipe would carry their thoughts and prayers to the Creator just as their Tobacco offerings in the fire would do.

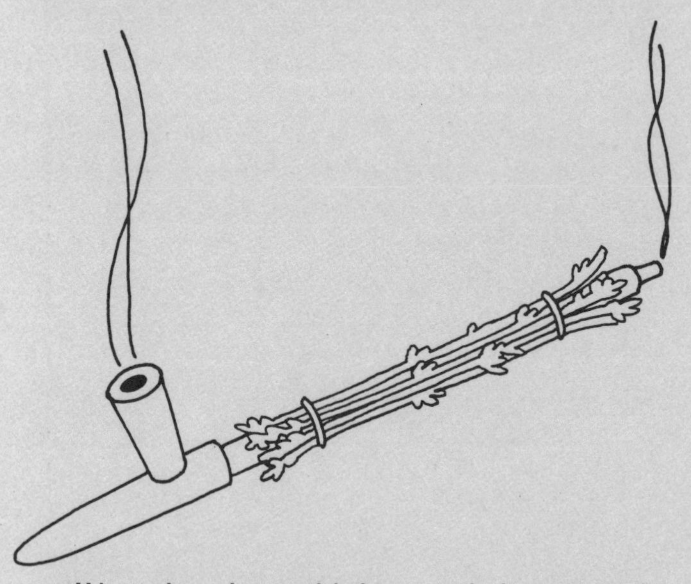

Waynaboozhoo told the people how to make the Pipe out of the sacred O-pwa'-gun-ah-sin' (pipestone) in the Earth and how to carve the pipestem from O-pwa'-gun-a-tig' (sumac).

With the coming of the Pipe, honor returned to be a guiding principle of life for many people. The sacredness of a person's word became, once again, foremost in day-to-day transactions.

The conflict and warfare subsided.

Still the seed was planted to use the Midewiwin and its spiritual powers for selfish concerns.

After some time, there came to be people who chose to use the Midewiwin as a way to build up their own personal power. They sought to instill fear in other people by harnessing spiritual powers and using them in evil ways. There were those that even took the lives of others and distorted the lives of their rivals by using their spiritual medicine in a bad way.

This was clearly against the intentions of the Creator. He was greatly angered at how such a beautiful gift could be so twisted and corrupted. The Creator instructed a very powerful spiritual being to destroy the Earth after the Sun rose four times. Some say that this being was the father of Waynaboozhoo. It looked as though all life on the Earth would be destroyed again.

Just before dawn on the fourth day, the Mi-gi-zi' (eagle) flew out of the crack between darkness and light — that edge between night and day. He flew straight into the sky. He flew so high that he flew completely out of sight. He flew to talk with the Creator. The Sun was about to come over the rim of the Earth. The eagle screamed four times to get the Creator's attention. The Creator saw the eagle and held back the Sun. At the time of this be-da'-bun ("false dawn"), the eagle talked to the Creator. He said, "I know the Earth is full of evil and corruption. I have seen all this. But also I have seen that there are yet a few people who have remained true to their instructions. I still see the smoke of Tobacco rise here and there from humble people who are still trying to live in harmony with the Universe. I plead on behalf of these few that you call off the destruction of the Earth. Let me fly over the Earth each day at dawn and look over the people. As long as I can report to you each day that there is still one person who sounds the Waterdrum or

The eagle flew to talk to the Creator.

who uses Tobacco and the Pipe in the proper way, I beg you to spare the Earth for the sake of the unborn. It is in these unborn that there is still hope for the Earth's people to correct their ways."

The Creator pondered what the eagle had to say. He then instructed the spiritual being in which he had left the destruction of the Earth to hold back his fury. He entrusted the eagle with the duty of reporting to him each day the condition of the Earth's people. The miracle of the sunrise happened again for the Anishinabe.

We owe our lives and the lives of our children to the eagle. This is why the eagle is so respected by native and natural people everywhere. This is why Indian people make a whistle from the wing-bone of the eagle. They sound this whistle four times at the start of their ceremonies. They do this to call in the power of the spirits. They do this to remember our brother, the eagle, and the role he plays in the preservation of the Earth.

Chapter 12

"The Sweat Lodge"

The old man who had visited the lodge of the Seven Grandfathers, brought back to the people the gift of seeking spiritual advice and direction through the Ba-wa'-ji-gay'-win (Vision Quest). As a child would approach the coming of adulthood, the parents would provide the opportunity for the child's first Vision Quest. Often a Mide'-wi-nini (Midewiwin priest) or Osh-ka-bay'-wis (helper) of the Midewiwin was asked to serve as a guide for the child. The body was deprived of food and water, the life-giving forces of physical life. With the physical side of life lessened, it was hoped that the spiritual side would come into dominance. It is also said that fasting purifies the body and the mind and makes a person receptive for messages coming from the Spirit World. If the child was ready and fortunate, a vision would come to serve as a guiding light in life. The vision would give life its purpose and direction.

It is told today of how once an Ojibway boy went on his first Vision Quest. He did not know what he was searching for. He did not know what answers he was seeking. On the fourth night of his fast, the boy's spirit was taken from his body. He traveled in spirit form straight toward the crescent Moon in the sky.

The boy traveled through four colors that are held around the Earth by a force Gitchie Manito placed on the Earth during the Creation. These colors stand for the Four Sacred Elements without which no life is possible. These four colors also stand for the four levels of spiritual knowledge that exist above the surface of the Earth.

The boy traveled through the part of the Moon that we cannot see — the part we know is there but which is dominated by the bright, shining crescent. The Moon is only whole when it is taken in its totality — that which we see and that we do not see. So is it with life. Life is not whole until its totality is comprehended. When the physical part of life that we can see is taken with the spiritual part of life that we do not so easily see, then life can be full and complete for each of us.

The boy traveled through the doorway of the crescent Moon and out into the Ah-nung'-go-kwan (Star World). He finally came to a lodge in

The boy traveled through the four colors held around the Earth and on to the doorway of the crescent Moon.

the sky. It was the lodge of Misho'-mis-i-non'-nig nee-zhwa'-swi (our Seven Grandfathers). Being much afraid, the boy cautiously looked inside. What he saw and felt can never be fully described or explained.

"Ha Be-in-di-gayn'! (Come in)" said one of the Grandfathers. "We have been expecting you. You have been sent to us by the Creator to carry a very special gift back to your people. We are going to instruct you in how a purifying ceremony can come to your people. It is a ceremony that will purify both the body and the mind."

The Grandfathers spoke as if their words were sent directly from their minds to the mind of the boy. They told the boy all the details as to how the ceremony should be performed:

"The lodge is to be made out of saplings from Pa-pa'-koo-si-gun' (the willow tree). The men of the village are responsible for gathering the willow and building the lodge. They should remember that before they take anything from the Earth in preparing the lodge that they are to offer Ah-say-ma' (Tobacco) in thanksgiving.

"The lodge is to have four doorways so that the spirits can enter from each of the Four Sacred Directions. Only the eastern doorway is to be used by humans. There should be four rings of willow placed around the framework of the lodge that represent the four levels of knowledge above the surface of the Earth. There are also four levels of knowledge below the surface of the Earth. All the saplings are to be lashed together with the inner bark of Wee-goo-bee' (the basswood tree).

"In the center of the lodge there shall be a shallow pit that will represent the o-nee-ja-win' (womb) of Mother Earth. The lodge will be covered with the skins of the deer, moose, buffalo, or with sheets of elm bark.

"Outside the lodge, a me-ka-naynz' (pathway) shall be made from the eastern doorway to the fireplace. The fireplace is to be surrounded by a crescent-shaped Ga'-ki-na wa-ji' bin-gwe' (altar).

"The menfolk shall be responsible for gathering rocks to place in the fire. If they put Tobacco down as an offering, they will be shown just what kind of rocks will withstand the intense heat of the fire.

"All these preparations including the gathering of firewood shall be done by the men. When their work is complete, the women of the village will prepare the grounds of the lodge for the ceremony. They shall carefully clean the Earth around the lodge, and with their hands give final shape to the crescent-shaped altar. Their final act will be to gather Gee-zhee-kan'-dug (Cedar) for the ceremony. The women will take some of this

Cedar and sprinkle it over the altar and down the pathway coming from the eastern door of the lodge.

"Certain ones of the menfolk will be honored with a position to hold or function to perform during the ceremony. The Na-gahn'-way-wi-nini (man who leads) of the ceremony will hold a very important but dangerous position. At the start of the ceremony he puts his life on the line for all those who will participate. His life can be taken by the Spirit World if anyone participating is harboring thoughts of hate or greed. He will be the keeper of the Waterdrum and the purifying water. He will sit just to the north side of the eastern doorway just as the spiritual keeper of the drum sits at the doorway of life. Next to him will sit the Ish-kwan-day'-wi-nini (Doorman) who will be responsible for directing the participants in the ceremony to their places and receiving the heated rocks from the Fireman. At the southern doorway of the lodge will sit the Birdman. In the western doorway will sit the Cedar Man. He will greet the ah-sin-neeg' (rocks) with offerings of Cedar. This western doorway is the doorway to the next world and to the future as well. In the northern doorway will sit Bearman. He sits in the place symbolic of purity, fasting, and the healing powers of Mother Earth. Each of these four men who occupy the four doorways will be offering their bodies for the spirits of the Four Directions to come through, speak through, and sing through. Their positions, too, occupy a very delicate and dangerous balance between the Spirit World and the physical world.

"The Ish-ko-day'-i-nini (Fireman) on the outside will occupy a vital position in that he will tend the fire and bring the heated rocks to the eastern door of the Ma-do-do-swun' (Sweat or Spirit Lodge). He first brings four rocks to be placed in the shallow pit of the lodge at each of the Four Directions. He then brings three rocks to make the four seven and to represent ourselves, the Seven Grandfathers. When the rocks are in their places in the lodge and the Doorman asks for the door to be closed, the ceremony begins when the Waterdrum is sounded four times. While the ceremony is in progress, the Fireman will tell all those on the outside of the lodge the origin of the ceremony and the symbolism of all the sacred things used. He will be responsible for educating the young Osh-ka-bay'-wi-sug (apprentices) who are helping and learning so that one day they too might earn a place in the Sweat Lodge.

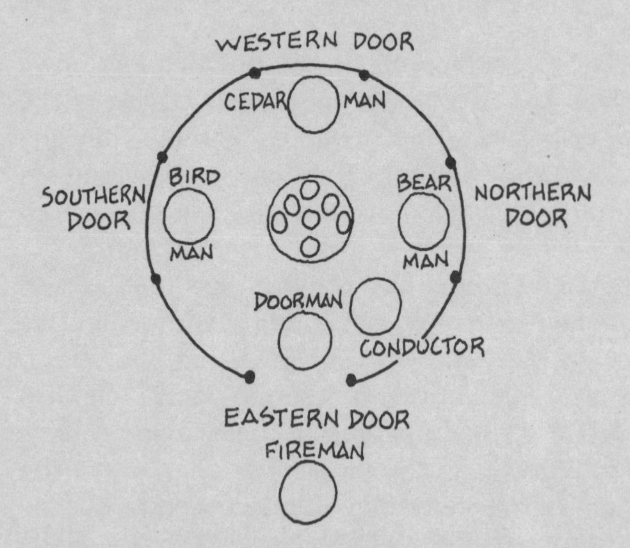

"If the conductor has been given the power through fasting or ceremony to conduct the Sweat Lodge for women, then a special ceremony can be held for the women of the village who have earned the right to sit in the lodge. The conductor will have to be very strong in order to hold a Sweat Lodge for the women. The women, with their life-giving powers, make the spiritual power of the Sweat Lodge very strong. They can make the spirit power so strong that a weak conductor might have difficulty in returning himself and the participants to the physical world at the end of the ceremony. Women can also be asked to hold a position at one of the doorways of the lodge."

The Seven Grandfathers gave the boy songs for the Sweat Lodge ceremony. They gave him songs for each of the Four Directions. They instructed him in all the details of the ceremony. They told him that the water which is offered to the heated rocks in the Sweat Lodge is capable of cleansing the bodies and minds of the people to make them pure and receptive for Spirit Ceremonies, Vision Quests, and the rigors of everyday life.

The Grandfathers told the boy that to sit next to the pit of rocks in the Sweat Lodge is like going back to your mother's womb. When the eastern doorway is opened and a person crawls humbly out into the world it is like being born anew. The pathway outside the eastern door represents the path of life. This pathway is sprinkled with the sacred medicine Cedar that we should use respectfully with all the other medicines to keep our bodies strong and pure in this life. The crescent shape of the altar represents the doorway of the Spirit World to which the origin of this ceremony is linked. And finally, the fire represents the very real power of the Spirit World — that hidden power that can be used to give balance to our lives.

The Seven Grandfathers then sent the boy back to Earth to carry this ceremony to his people.

When the boy awoke, he found that he was too weak to move. He did not know where he was. He was finally able to reach out with his fingers and clutch at some plant brothers and sisters that were growing next to him. With much effort he brought his hand to his mouth. It was Cedar that was growing around him. He ate some of the Cedar and it gave him strength.

After a while he was able to sit up. He found himself on top of a chi-wa-jiw' (mountain). He tried to remember the details of his vision but he could not. As he looked from side to side he discovered that the mountain on which he was sitting was shaped like a huge Oh-shka-goon-jing' gee'-sis (crescent Moon). Suddenly, parts of his vision came back to him and he remembered the altar of the Sweat Lodge. He noticed that Cedar was growing all around him on the mountain just as the Grandfathers told him Cedar should be sprinkled on the altar of the Sweat Lodge.

At the moment of his awakening, it was dawn here on the Earth — the brief time before the Sun comes over the rim of the Earth. As the Sun rose up behind him he noticed a fire burning with rocks in it below him in the valley. As the Sun rose his shadow seemed to make a path through the center of the fire and beyond to a lodge that stood there exactly as it appeared in his vision. He remembered that the altar was to be placed to the East of the Sweat Lodge just as the mountain on which he was sitting was located to the East of the fire and lodge below. Looking to the West in the valley below, he was amazed to see that the lodge, fire and the altar-like mountain were in perfect alignment with himself and the new day Sun.

The rekindled memory of his time with the Seven Grandfathers gave the boy strength he had never known before. He came to his feet, placed Tobacco on the Earth for all that he had been given, and began the long walk home holding inside of him a very special gift for the people.

This is the teaching that was given to the Ojibway to tell how the purification ceremony or Sweat Lodge came to our people. Remember that the other nations and tribes were given teachings that are slightly different from this. But in all the teachings of different tribes there is a commonality. This sameness refers to the basic Truth that interweaves all natural ways of living.

Today, the Sweat Lodge is still used by groups of traditional people who choose to lead a natural way of life. The ceremony has kept its original form through the years. Many of the songs used today go back hundreds of years. Today, canvas is predominantly used to cover the Sweat Lodge but there are still those who make permanent lodges using elm bark as a covering. The elm bark can only be gathered in the spring when the bark can be peeled easily from the tree.

It is good that in spite of all the changes that modern life has brought to Indian people, that there are those who keep strong the gifts of yesterday. For it is with yesterday that we learn for tomorrow.

Chapter 13

The Seven Fires

The accounts of our life that have been handed down to us by our Ojibway elders tell us that many years ago, seven major nee-gawn-na-kayg' (prophets) came to the Anishinabe. They came at a time when the people were living a full and peaceful life on the northeastern coast of North America. These prophets left the people with seven predictions of what the future would bring. Each of these prophecies was called a Fire and each Fire referred to a particular era of time that would come in the future. Thus, the teachings of the seven prophets are now called the Neesh-wa-swi' ish-ko-day-kawn' (Seven Fires) of the Ojibway.

The first prophet said to the people, "In the time of the First Fire, the Anishinabe nation will rise up and follow the Sacred Shell of the Midewiwin Lodge. The Midewiwin Lodge will serve as a rallying point for the people and its traditional ways will be the source of much strength. The Sacred Megis will lead the way to the chosen ground of the Anishinabe. You are to look for a turtle-shaped island that is linked to the purification of the Earth. You will find such an island at the beginning and end of your journey. There will be seven stopping places along the way. You will

know that the chosen ground has been reached when you come to a land where food grows on water. If you do not move, you will be destroyed."

The second prophet told the people, "You will know the Second Fire because at this time the nation will be camped by a large body of water. In this time the direction of the Sacred Shell will be lost. The Midewiwin will diminish in strength. A boy will be born to point the way back to the traditional ways. He will show the direction to the stepping stones to the future of the Anishinabe people."

The third prophet said to the people, "In the Third Fire, the Anishinabe will find the path to their chosen ground, a land in the West to which they must move their families. This will be the land where food grows on water."

The Fourth Fire was originally given to the people by two prophets. They came as one. They told of the coming of the Light-skinned Race.

One of the prophets said, "You will know the future of our people by what face the Light-skinned Race wears. If they come wearing the face of nee-kon'-nis-i-win' (brotherhood), then there will come a time of wonderful change for

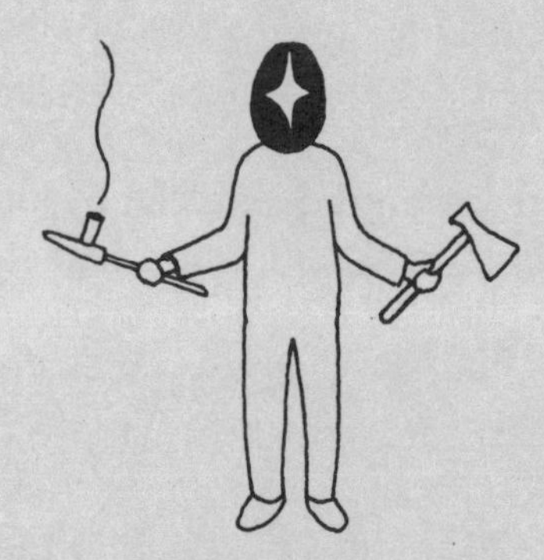

generations to come. They will bring new knowledge and articles that can be joined with the knowledge of this country. In this way two nations will join to make a mighty nation. This new nation will be joined by two more so that the four will form the mightiest nation of all. You will know the face of brotherhood if the Light-skinned Race comes carrying no weapons, if they come bearing only their knowledge and a handshake."

The other prophet said, "Beware if the Light-skinned Race comes wearing the face of ni-boo-win′ (death). You must be careful because the face of brotherhood and the face of death look very much alike. If they come carrying a weapon . . . beware. If they come in suffering . . . they could fool you. Their hearts may be filled with greed for the riches of this land. If they are indeed your brothers, let them prove it. Do not accept them in total trust. You shall know that the face they wear is the one of death if the rivers run with poison and fish become unfit to eat. You shall know them by these many things."

The fifth prophet said, "In the time of the Fifth Fire there will come a time of great struggle that will grip the lives of all Native people. At the waning of this Fire there will come among the people one who holds a promise of great joy and salvation. If the people accept this promise of a new way and abandon the old teachings, then the struggle of the Fifth Fire will be with the people for many generations. The promise that comes will prove to be a false promise. All those who accept this promise will cause the near destruction of the people."

The prophet of the Sixth Fire said, "In the time of the Sixth Fire it will be evident that the promise of the Fifth Fire came in a false way. Those deceived by this promise will take their children away from the teachings of the chi′-ah-ya-og′ (elders). Grandsons and granddaughters will turn against the elders. In this way the elders will lose their reason for living . . . they will lose their purpose in life. At this time a new sickness will come among the people. The balance of many people will be disturbed. The cup of life will almost be spilled. The cup of life will almost become the cup of grief."

At the time of these predictions, many people scoffed at the prophets. They then had mush-kee-ki′-wi-nun′ (medicines) to keep away sickness. They were then healthy and happy as a people. These were the people who chose to stay behind on the great migration of the Anishinabe. These people were the first to have contact with the Light-skinned Race. They would suffer the most.

When the Fifth Fire came to pass, a great struggle did indeed grip the lives of all Native people. The Light-skinned Race launched a military attack on Indian people throughout the country aimed at taking away their land and their independence as a free and sovereign people. It is now felt that the false promise that came at the end of the Fifth Fire was the materials and riches embodied in the way of life of the Light-skinned Race. Those who abandoned the ancient ways and accepted this new promise were a big factor in causing the near-destruction of the Native people of this land.

When the Sixth Fire came to be, the words of the prophet rang true as children were taken away from the teachings of the elders. The boarding school era of "civilizing" Indian children had begun. The Indian language and religion were taken from the children. The people starting dying at an early age . . . they had lost their will to live and their purpose in living.

In the confusing times of the Sixth Fire, it is said that a group of visionaries came among the Anishinabe. They gathered all the priests of the Midewiwin Lodge. They told the priests that the Midewiwin Way was in danger of being destroyed. They gathered all the sacred bundles. They gathered all the Wee'-gwas scrolls that recorded the ceremonies. All these things were placed in a hollowed-out log from Ma-none' (the ironwood tree). Men were lowered over a cliff by long ropes. They dug a hole in the cliff and buried the log where no one could find it. Thus the teachings of the elders were hidden out of sight but not out of memory. It was said that when the time came that Indian people could practice their religion without fear that a little boy would dream where the ironwood log full of sacred bundles and scrolls was buried. He would lead his people to the place.

The seventh prophet that came to the people long ago was said to be different from the other prophets. He was young and had a strange light in his eyes. He said, "In the time of the Seventh Fire a Osh-ki-bi-ma-di-zeeg' (New People) will emerge. They will retrace their steps to find what

In the time of the Seventh Fire a New People will emerge to retrace their steps to find what was left by the trail.

was left by the trail. Their steps will take them to the elders who they will ask to guide them on their journey. But many of the elders will have fallen asleep. They will awaken to this new time with nothing to offer. Some of the elders will be silent out of fear. Some of the elders will be silent because no one will ask anything of them. The New People will have to be careful in how they approach the elders. The task of the New People will not be easy.

"If the New People will remain strong in their quest, the Waterdrum of the Midewiwin Lodge will again sound its voice. There will be a rebirth of the Anishinabe nation and a rekindling of old flames. The Sacred Fire will again be lit.

"It is at this time that the Light-skinned Race will be given a choice between two roads. If they choose the right road, then the Seventh Fire will light the Eighth and Final Fire — an eternal Fire of peace, love, brotherhood and sisterhood. If the Light-skinned Race makes the wrong choice of roads, then the destruction which they brought with them in coming to this country will come back to them and cause much suffering and death to all the Earth's people."

Traditional Mide people of Ojibway and people from other nations have interpreted the "two roads" that face the Light-skinned Race as the road to technology and road to spiritualism. They feel that the road to technology represents a continuation of the head-long rush to technological development. This is the road that has led modern society to a damaged and seared Earth. Could it be that the road to technology represents a rush to destruction? The road to spirituality represents the slower path that traditional Native people have traveled and are now seeking again. The Earth is not scorched on this trail. The grass is still growing there.

The prophet of the Fourth Fire spoke of a time when "two nations will join to make a mighty nation." He was speaking of the coming of the Light-skinned Race and the face of brotherhood that the Light-skinned brother could be wearing. It is obvious from the history of this country that this was not the face worn by the Light-skinned Race as a whole. That mighty nation spoken of in the Fourth Fire has never been formed.

If we natural people of the Earth could just wear the face of brotherhood, we might be able to deliver our society from the road to destruction. Could we make the two roads that today represent two clashing world views come together to form that mighty nation? Could a nation be formed that is guided by respect for all living things?

Are we the New People of the Seventh Fire?

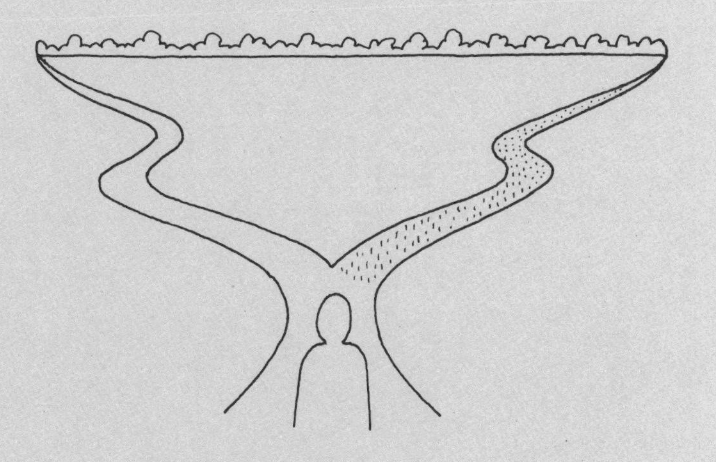

Chapter 14

The Migration of the Anishinabe

Boozhoo, I am going to try to reconstruct the chi-bi-moo-day-win′ (migration) of my Ojibway ancestors. I will draw upon the words given to us by the prophets of the Seven Fires. I have also looked at old maps of North America that might give hints to places referred to by the seven prophets and by my grandfathers. Finally, I have listened to what the scholars have had to say about early written accounts of this country.

When the seven prophets came to the Anishinabe, the nation was living somewhere on the shores of the Great Salt Water in the East. There are many opinions about where this settlement was. It is generally agreed that the Ojibways and other Algonquin Indians were settled up and down the eastern shores of North America. We have some idea of the size of the nation from these words that have been handed down: "The people were so many and powerful that if one was to climb the highest mountain and look in all directions, they would not be able to see the end of the nation." Bands and clans were scattered here and there. There were berry pickers, wood carvers, fishermen, canoe makers, and stone carvers. There were those who were charged with raising food from Mother Earth. They were called the Gi-ti-gay′-wi-nini-wug′ (planters or keepers of the Creator's garden). There was an active ex-

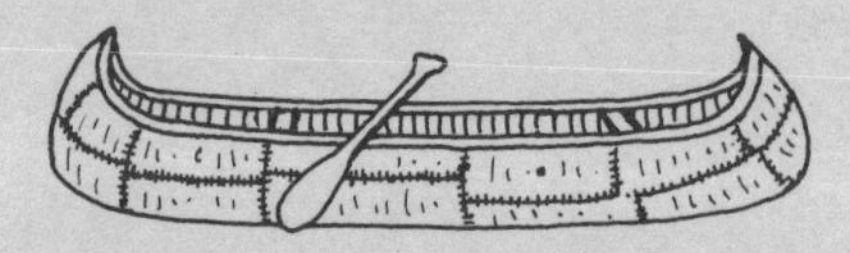

change and communication among all the groups of people. They used the waterways of the land to travel by canoe. They had a system of overland trails. They used sleds and dog teams to travel in the winter. Life was full for the people here. The Clan System and its government were strongly enforced. There was ample food from the land and sea, and there were fish from many rivers.

This fullness of life made many people doubt the predictions of the seven prophets. There was much discussion among all the Anishinabe about the migration and the prophecies of the Seven Fires. Huge gatherings were held to discuss the plans of the nation. Many people did not want to move their families on the journey to the West. Others were ready to follow the believers in the migration and give their unselfish support to what they felt was the Creator's plan. There was one group who supported the migration but who pledged to remain at the eastern doorway and care for the eastern fire of the people. They were called the Wa-bun-u-keeg′ or Daybreak People.

Today, it is speculated that these were the people living on the east coast of Canada that the French called the Abnaki.

The prophet of the First Fire had told the people: "If you do not move, you will be destroyed." It would come to pass that most all those who stayed behind, including the Daybreak People, were destroyed or absorbed by the Light-skinned Race at the coming of the Fourth Fire.

The Mide people remembered the words of the prophet of the First Fire. He had spoken of a turtle-shaped mi-ni-si' (island) that would be the first of seven stopping places during the migration.

Some people thought that this island of the beginning of their journey was surely a place of great power and that they were to go there and await further instructions from the Creator. Others thought that those who accepted the words of the prophets should seek out this island and go there for Sweat Lodge and purification ceremonies. Still others felt that the search for the island was a test of their strength by Gitchie Manito. There was a great search throughout all the waters of the land for this island.

At last, a woman who was carrying a child in her womb had a ba-wa-zi-gay-win' (dream). In this dream she found herself standing on the back of a turtle in the water. The tail of the turtle pointed to the direction of the rising Sun and its head faced the West. The turtle was in a river that ran into the setting Sun.

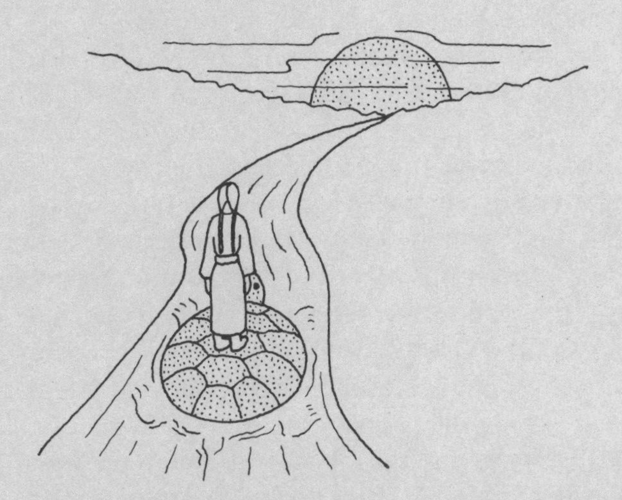

The woman told her husband of her dream. Her husband took the dream to the old men of the Midewiwin Lodge. These elders accepted this dream in its totality and instructed the people to explore the rivers in search of such an island.

Such an island was finally found in the St. Lawrence River. There has been much discussion today as to where this first stopping place of the migration was located. There is a place a short way northeast of present-day Montreal where the St. Francis River runs into the southern shore of the St. Lawrence. This is the only river of the region that flows to the West. At the place where this river joins the St. Lawrence there is a small island. Many years ago, the French found a fairly large Indian village on the mainland just across from the island. This island fits the description of the turtle-shaped island in the woman's dream.

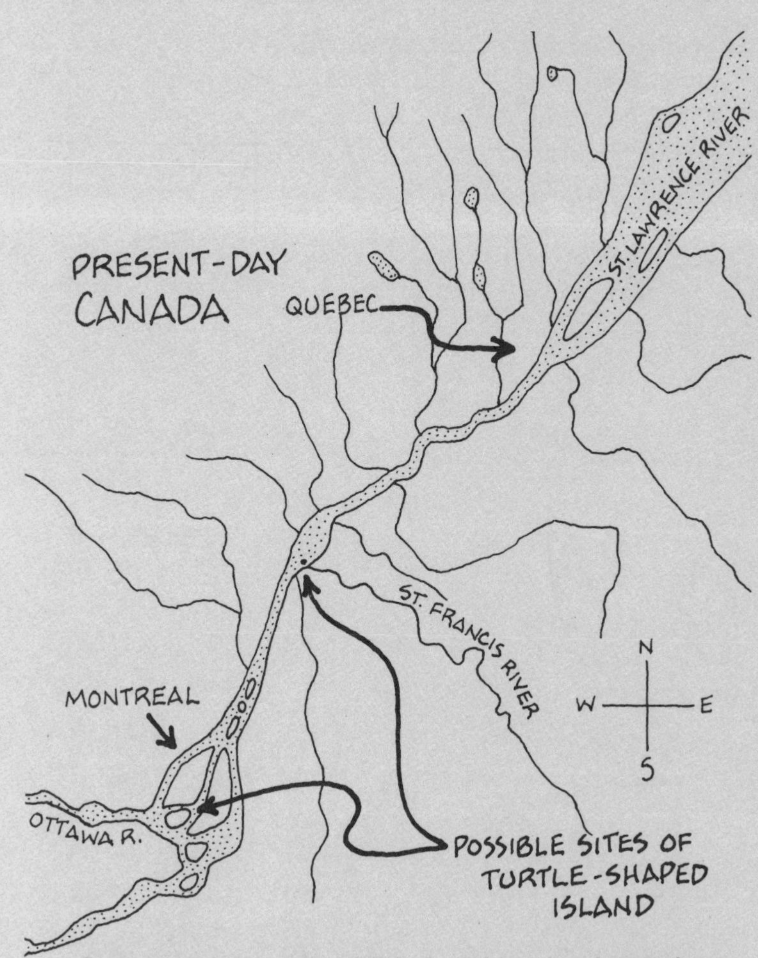

Some people today think that this island was the first stopping place of the migration. Others have pointed to a small island just where the Ottawa River joins the St. Lawrence at Montreal. The Ottawa River runs in line with the path of the Sun but it flows to the East.

It is likely that the main body of the migration camped on and around one of these islands. There were many Spirit Ceremonies and cleansing ceremonies held there as the people sought additional instructions.

After some time, the people resumed their journey to the West. They were told that along their journey they would have to stand and protect themselves from harassment and pursuit by other nations. They knew if they could stay true to the teachings of the Midewiwin that they would remain strong. The Anishinabe knew that they were to honor all and fear none. They were not to advocate war or violence, but when faced with conflict, they were not to shrink from it.

One of the major adversaries of the migrating Anishinabe was called the Nah-du-wayg.′ They were the Six Nations that made up the Iroquois Confederacy.

Along the migration there was a group of men who were charged with keeping the Manido ish-ko-day′ (Sacred Fire). It was a flame that should never be allowed to die. The Sacred Fire gave strength to the warriors and kept the people of the migration together. All the campfires of the people were to come from the coals of this Sacred Fire. In this way continuity was given to the lives of the Anishinabe.

There were family groups and clan groups that differed in the interpretations of the prophecies. Some of these groups decided to stop along the way of the migration and set up permanent camps for their followers. It was said that from the head of the migration where the Waterdrum and Pipe were carried, the campfires of all the Anishinabe and their offshoots lit the landscape at night like stars for as far as the eye could see. Those that stayed behind were given their own flame of the original Sacred Fire.

It is now thought that the people slowly moved down the southern shore of the St. Lawrence River. Their second major stopping place was at the Ani-mi-kee′ wa-bu (the place of the Thunder Water). This is very likely the place referred to by Waynaboozhoo on his journey to find his father

The Ojibway followed the direction of the Sacred Shell on their migration.

and the place the the Ojibway later called Kichi-ka-be-kong' (Great Falls). The water and thunder came together here and made a powerful place. When the people stopped here, the Sacred Megis Shell rose up out of the water and greeted them. The Sacred Fire was moved to this location for some time. This place is better known today as Niagara Falls.

From here, the people moved to a place identified by one of the earlier prophets as "a place where two great bodies of water are connected by a thin, narrow river." This river was described as a "deep and fast ribbon of water that slices through the land like a knife." Many lives were lost in crossing this river. This third stopping place was very likely the shores of the Detroit River that connects Lake St. Clair and Lake Huron in the North to Lake Erie in the South. It is said that again the Sacred Megis appeared to the people out of the water.

It was at this second stopping place that the Anishinabe drove back a large group of Iroquois warriors who were pursuing them. Later, the Iroquois gave the Ojibway a Wampum Belt made out of a very special kind of shell. The O-pwa'-gun (Pipe) was shared among these two nations. At last peace was sealed between them.

In this period, three groups began to emerge in the Ojibway nation. Each group took upon themselves certain tasks necessary for the survival of the people. There came to be a very strong spiritual sense that bound these groups together.

The group called the Ish-ko-day'-wa-tomi (fire people) were charged with the safekeeping of the Sacred Fire. As the people moved on the migration, this group guarded the coals of the Sacred Fire as it was carried along. These people were later called the O-day'-wa-tomi, and, still later, the Potawatomi.

The group called the O-daw-wahg' (trader people) were responsible for providing food goods and supplies to all the nation. They took charge of the major hunting and trading expeditions. These people were later called the Ottawa.

The people that retained the name Ojibway were the faith keepers of the nation. They were entrusted with the keeping of the sacred scrolls and Waterdrum of the Midewiwin. These people were later mistakenly referred to as the Chippewa.

All the Anishinabe people became known as the nation of the Three Fires to recognize how these groups provided for all their needs.

There were those among the Three Fires that were known as peace makers. Others spoke out for military preparations to protect the nation. Still others felt the purpose of the Three Fires was to see that the prophesies were fulfilled. Huge gatherings of the Three Fires were held to discuss all of these things and decide on future actions.

By necessity, the alliance grew in military strength, but never was the spiritual origin and purpose of the Three Fires forgotten or

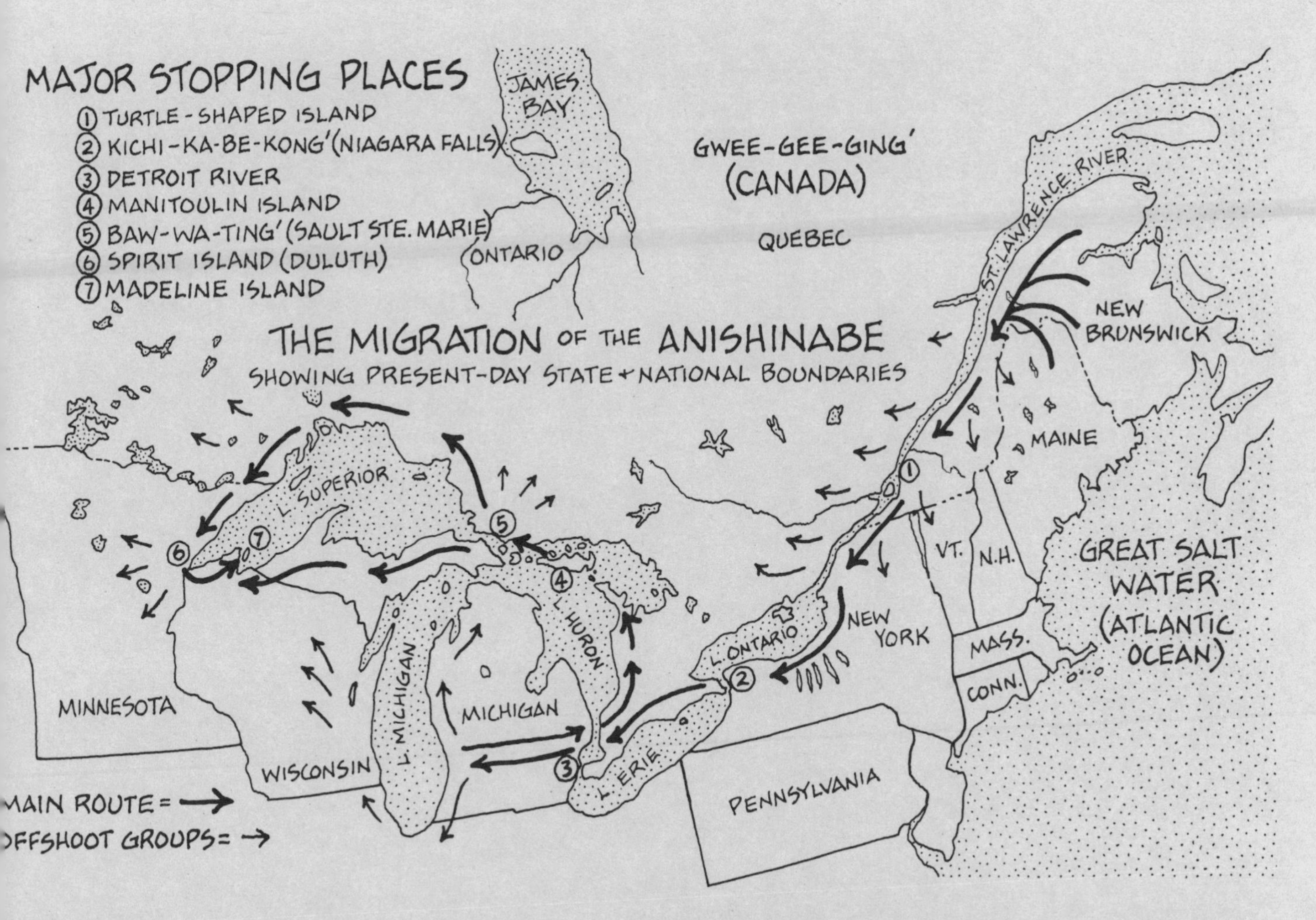

abandoned.

The Three Fires were later courted heavily by Indian leaders from East to join combat expeditions against the Light-skinned Race. Certain ones responded to these requests but never was there a massive military effort on the part of the Three Fires. If the entire strength of the Three Fires had been focused on military actions, then the history of this country would most certainly be different.

The people picked up the Waterdrum and continued their westward journey. They were attacked along the way by the nations later called the Sauks and the Foxes. The people pushed on until they came to a large body of fresh water. Here, the Sacred Fire rested for a long time. This is the place that was referred to in the prophecy of the Second Fire. It is possible that this camping place of the migration was on the eastern shore of Lake Michigan. At this point many people drifted off by groups to look for a place to cross the great water. They knew that their journey must take them to the West, but some of the people traveled South in an attempt to go around the water. Many felt that the direction of the migration had become lost and that the people had missed their fourth stopping place. Time passed so that there were many births and deaths among the people. Giti-gan-nug' (gardens) were raised and o-day-na-wing' (villages) were established. As related in the Second Fire, people began to wander away from the teachings of the Midewiwin Lodge. Many became preoccupied with satisfying the things needed for physical survival but neglected the spiritual side of life. Many lost the direction in their lives that comes from Spirit Ceremony and Sweat Lodge. Only a few of the people, mostly elders, were able to keep the Sacred Fire alive. But the prophecies said that "a boy would be born to show the Anishinabe back to the sacred ways." It was prophesied that he would show the way to "the stepping stones to the future of the Anishinabe people." That boy did come among the people. He had a dream of stones that led across the water. The Mide people paid attention to this dream and led the people back to the river that cut the land like a knife. They followed the river to the North. The river turned into a lake, and at a place where the river was formed again, they rested awhile on an island. This island is known today as Walpole Island. They continued following the river further and came to the northern sea of freshwater that they had heard about when they first came to this region. They followed its eastern shore until, at last, they discovered a series of islands that led across the water. By moving the people by canoe, a way was found to the West over these "stepping stones." And so, the prophecy of the Third Fire came true for the people. They found "the path to their chosen ground, a land in the West to which they must move their families." Here they would find "the food that grows on water."

On the largest island in this chain, the Sacred Megis appeared to the Anishinabe. Here the people gathered. This is the island known today as Manitoulin Island. Slowly, the Anishinabe gathered until Manitoulin Island became known as the capital of the Ojibway nation. Here, the Midewiwin Way grew in following and the Clan System flourished. Truly, the boy with the dream did lead the people back to the sacred ways. Manitoulin Island became the fourth major stopping place of the migration. It is said that the voice of the Waterdrum could be heard even several days journey from Manitoulin Island.

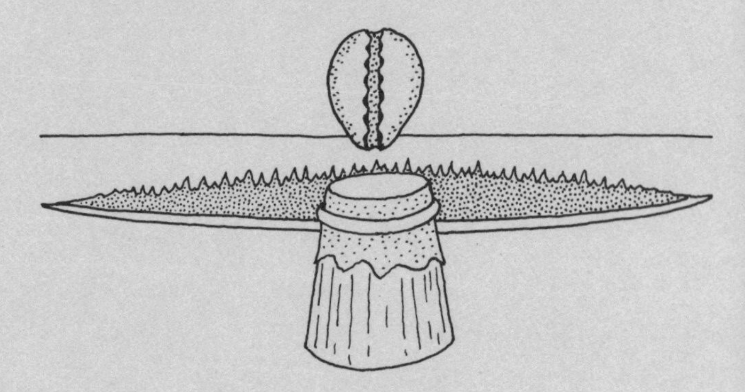

For some time the main body of the migration stayed on this island, but it was not until the people settled at Baw-wa-ting' that the Waterdrum was given a home in which to rest and sing. Here again, the people found the Megis Shell. There was a small island here where powerful ceremonies were held. People now call this place Sault Ste. Marie. The fishing was excellent in the fast water. Skilled fishermen could run the rapids with a canoe while standing backwards in the bow. They would be carrying an ah-sub-bi' (net) on the end of a long pole. By the

time they got to the quiet water of the river, their canoe would be full of beautiful Mi-ti-goo-ka-maig' (whitefish). There was so much food in the village that this place came to support many families. Baw-wa-ting' became the fifth stopping place of the migration. Many years later, in the time of the Fifth Fire, Baw-wa-ting' would become a big trading center between the Anishinabe and the Light-skinned Race.

From Baw-wa-ting', the migration split into two large groups. One group followed the shore of another great body of water to the West. The other group followed the northern shore. Both of these groups were attacked by the people they called Ba-wahn.' They were called this to denote their way of talking in deep voices. Their hunting territory was being invaded by the migrating newcomers and they fought fiercely. These conflicts illustrate the way that both of these nations were devoted to their purposes in life. The Ba-wahn' were later called Dakotas by the Light-skinned Race.

The northern group of Anishinabe carved muz-i-nee-bi' ah-sin' (rock markings) and symbols on the huge rock cliffs that led down to the great water. They marked sacred places and made records of their journey on the rock walls. They

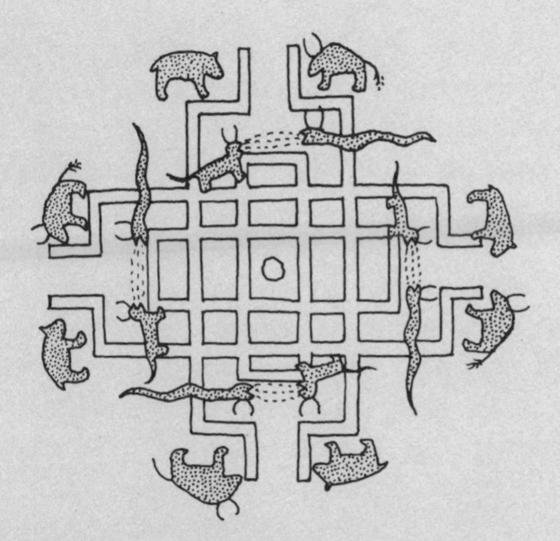

went all the way to the western end of the water. They named the bay there Wee-kway-doung'. Here they settled on an island. The Sacred Shell rose up to the people from the sands of its shore. This island today is referred to as Spirit Island at the west end of Lake Superior. Parts of the southern group came to this place, too. They also left carvings on the rocks along the southern shore of Lake Superior. It was near Spirit Island that the words of the prophets were fulfilled. Here the Anishinabe found "the food that grows on water." Here they found Ma-no'-min (wild rice).

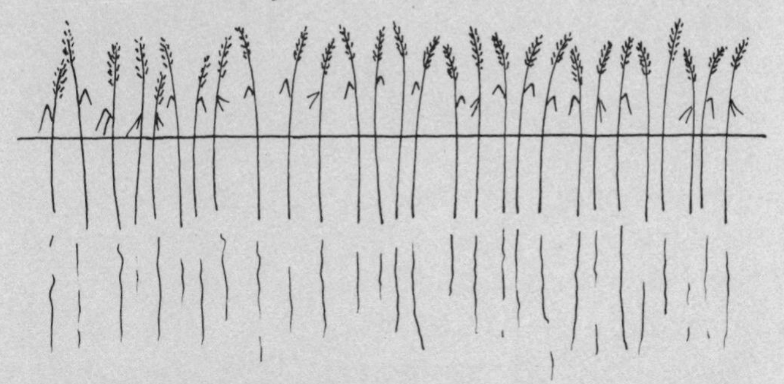

Wild rice has always been regarded by the Ojibway as the sacred gift of their chosen ground. Any effort today to over-harvest or commercialize wild rice has met with failure. Wild rice has always been generous to those who gather and use her in a respectful way.

This island in the bay became the sixth major stopping place of the migration. The elders of the Midewiwin Lodge sensed that the long journey of their people was near its end. But something was missing. One of the prophets long ago had spoken of a turtle-shaped island that awaited them at the end of their journey. The southern group had seen an island fitting this description that lay in the water off of a long point of land. The people sought out this island and placed tobacco on its shore. The Sacred Shell rose up out of the water and told the people that this was the place they had been searching for. Here, the Waterdrum made its seventh and final stop on the migration. The Sacred Fire was carried here and here it burned brightly. This island was called Mo-ning-wun′-a-kawn-ing (the place that was dug) by the Ojibway. It was later called Madeline Island. This name has survived to this day. The main body of the Anishinabe people gathered here and they became strong and powerful.

At last the migration to the chosen ground was at an end. It is thought that the migration started around 900 A.D. It took some 500 years to complete. It is amazing that the Sacred Fire could be kept alive for so long. The dream of the original seven prophets was carried for many generations. It was carried along a string of fires with many campfires left behind. That the people were able to accomplish such a thing is truly a miracle of the Creator.

We descendents of these great people can gather strength from their strength. We can gather courage for our lives today from their courage of yesterday.

Chapter 15

Conclusion: Stepping Into Modern History

Nokomis and I would like to thank you for joining us for these teachings of the Ojibway. We feel very good that you have honored us with your presence for so long. We ended our last teaching by following the migration of the Ojibway to their final stopping place on Madeline Island in Lake Superior.

The huge settlement of Ojibways on Madeline Island was a springboard to the future of the people. Outside of occasional skirmishes with the Dakota people, the Ojibways lived for many years in peace on Madeline Island. The Midewiwin Lodge gained a strength and following that had never been known before. The Midewiwin sought to tap guidance and help from the Spirit World, from the four-leggeds that it honored, and from the healing beings of the plant world. The people had truly found the joy of living that comes from existing in harmony with all the forces of the Four Directions and the Universe.

One of the chiefs on Madeline Island kept a special o-za-wa-bik' (copper medallion) in his sacred Mide bundle. The medallion was carefully made by his grandfathers from a copper deposit found on the shore of Lake Superior. His grandfathers had carved a notch on the edge of the medallion when the Ojibway first settled on Madeline Island. The medallion was then kept by a member of the family until he or she passed into the Spirit World. Then the medallion was handed down to one of the members of the younger generation. A new notch was carved on the medallion and it was carried again for another lifetime. In this way a record was kept of the generations of Ojibway that lived on Madeline Island.

By the third notch carved on the copper disc was also inscribed the figure of a man wearing a large hat. It is believed that this represents the time in which the Ojibway of Madeline Island first heard of the arrival of the long-awaited Light-skinned Race. It is likely that the Ojibways of Madeline Island heard this news on visits to the homes of their relatives at Baw-wa-ting' (Sault Ste. Marie). The people of Baw-wa-ting' would often go on long trading journeys back along the trail of the migration. It is even said that they traded with the Wa-bun-u-keeg' (Daybreak People) who stayed behind on the migration at the eastern doorway. It is very likely that these traders were the ones that brought the news of the Light-skinned Race back to the Great Lakes area.

It was many years before the Light-skinned Race actually came to the western Great Lakes. They came first in the form of explorers from the nation of France seeking to know the riches of the northern forests. One of the first French explorers to come into this area was named Brule. In 1618 he returned to the French settlement in Quebec with the first description of Lake Superior.

On the wake of the explorers came ah-daway'-wi-ni-neeg' (traders) from the French nation. They came bearing gifts of good will. They brought metal axes, steel knives, kettles and cooking pots of iron, beautiful woven cloth, coats and other articles of clothing, and colored glass beads. The French traders sought not only the

The French traders were among the first of the Light-skinned Race to appear among the Ojibways.

good will of the Native people, they sought the furs of the otter, beaver, fox, ermine, and others of the four-leggeds. These traders lived a rough life. They referred to themselves as "voyageurs" because of the long journeys that they would make each year soon after the rivers and lakes were free of ice. They traveled by wee-gwas'-i-jee-mon' (birchbark canoe). They would sometimes have to carry their canoes, provisions, and trade goods over long portages between lakes or around dangerous rapids.

To the Ojibway of Madeline Island, the French traders seemed to come wearing the face of brotherhood. They seemed genuinely friendly and respectful. Perhaps this was because of their closeness to the Earth and her waterways. The Ojibway accepted these traders as brothers. The Ojibway were so sincere in their acceptance that they adopted some of these French people into their nation. Some of the French traders took Ojibway wives. Since the Clan System worked on the basis of assigning the children of a marriage to the clan of their father, the Ojibways adopted these special Frenchmen into the wa-bi-zha-shi'-do-i-daym' (Martin Clan), the clan of the warriors. In this way the children of the Frenchmen were given a clan. It was possibly felt that the acceptance of the responsibilities of this clan would be a worthy test of the sincerity of the newcomers. The French traders must have impressed the Ojibway with their loyalty because they were accepted, for the most part, fully and completely. In their generosity and innocence the Ojibway did not know of the wave of foreigners that was already beginning to form in their old homeland on the east coast of North America.

One of these French traders set up a trading post on Madeline Island in the early 1800's. His name was Michael Cadotte. He took an Ojibway wife and raised a family. One of his daughters married a man named Lyman Warren and they continued the trading business since Michael was getting on in his years. Their son William became a historian and talked to an Ojibway elder in 1844 who had kept the copper medallion that we spoke of earlier. At this time there were eight notches on the edge of the disc. Sure enough, the picture of the man wearing the big hat was carved by the third notch. The old Ojibway man died shortly after this and another notch was added to the medallion.

Just for speculation's sake, if we took the lifetime of an Ojibway in these old days to be 50 years, counting backwards it would put the coming of the news of the Light-skinned Race to this area at 1544 and the settlement of the Ojibway on Madeline Island at 1394. This is just a guess but it does give us some idea of how these accounts fit into historical development of this country.

The next foreigners to come into the western Great Lakes were called Muk-a-day'-i-ko-na-yayg' ("the Black Coats") by the Ojibway. They came carrying a cross similar to representations of the Four Sacred Directions. They wore long black robes and held a black book very close to their hearts.

The Black Coats came from the Jesuit Order of the Catholic Church and many of them admired the way the Ojibway tried to live in harmony with all parts of the Creation. They were struck most by the generosity of the Native people and the honor associated with one's word. Some of the missionaries were even afraid for the Indian people in what lay ahead for them in their exposure to the corrupt world of the new European settlers.

For the most part, however, the Ojibways found the Black Coats to be less respectful of their way of life as compared to the respect shown by the French traders. Some of the Black Coats served as spies for the French military by informing them of the location and strength of Indian villages. Often the Black Coats seemed to be obsessed with winning the Native people over to the ways of their black book. The Black Coats said that it was necessary for the Ojibway people to know the teachings of a prophet named "Jesus" from another land. If they did not accept these teachings, they would not pass on to join their ancestors in the Spirit World to the West. Instead, they would burn forever in a place under the ground! This idea was terrifying to many Native people.

The Black Coats and their Indian converts seemed bent on dividing up the Ojibway villages into factions. The Christian Indians were encouraged to resent and reject the followers of the Midewiwin Lodge.

Finally, this factionalism found its way to the Ojibway settlement on Madeline Island. It was about this time that the followers of the Midewiwin were accused of devil-worship and cannibalism. It is possible that some misguided individuals might have attempted to use mud-ji' mush-kee-ki' ("bad medicine") on rival factions in the community. At any rate the Ojibway settlement on Madeline Island began to break up. One large group left the island and journeyed south into the mainland until they came to a huge lake. On the shores of this lake they found the frozen body of an Indian. They put his body to rest with a Tobacco offering. They took this discovery to be a powerful sign, and, not far from this spot, they established a village. This place was called

Lac Courte Oreille (Lake of the Short Ears) by the French. Another group left Madeline Island and settled a short way off at a place thereafter called Red Cliff. One group moved a little further away and set up a village called Odanah. They were called the Bad River Ojibways. Still other groups left the Madeline Island settlement. There were groups that, themselves, split into different factions. An Ojibway community was established at a place called Sand Lake, Wisconsin. Later, an offshoot of this village formed another community at Round Lake, Wisconsin. The state that is now known as Minnesota was and still is home of many bands of Ojibway that came directly from Madeline Island or from earlier offshoots of

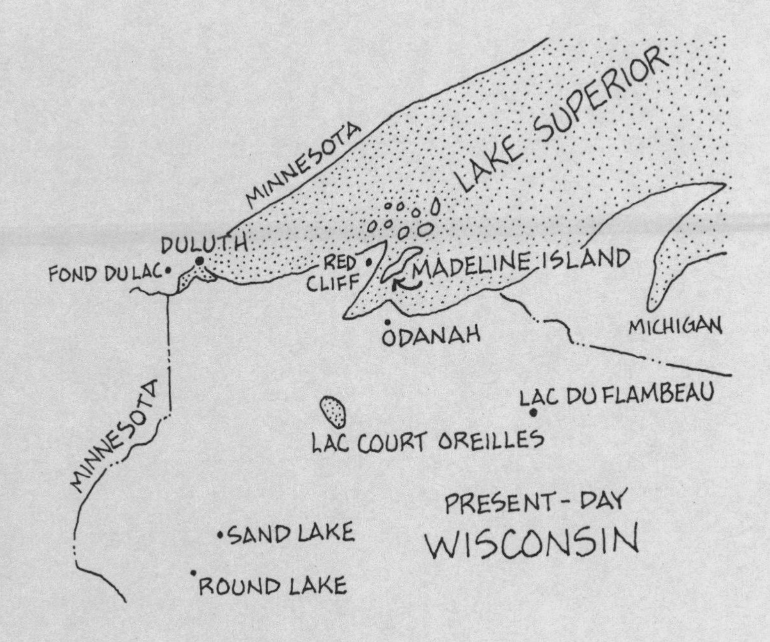

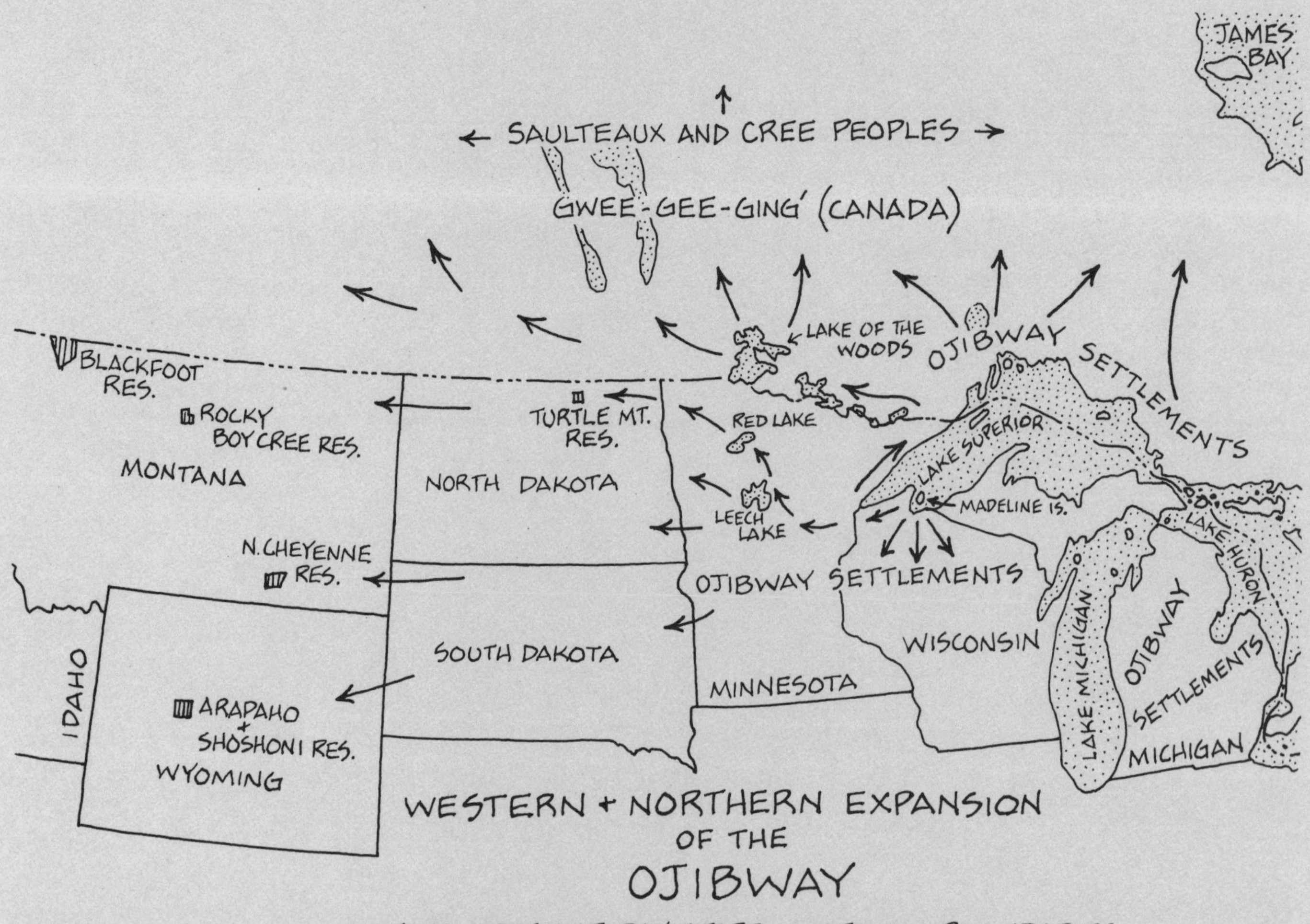

WESTERN + NORTHERN EXPANSION OF THE OJIBWAY

USING PRESENT-DAY STATE + NATIONAL BOUNDARIES

the Migration. The Ojibways settled all around the shores of Lake Superior. Many of these villages on the north shore became part of Gwee-gee-ging' (Canada) after the War of 1812. Ojibways and their relatives pushed as far west as what is now called the Turtle Mountain Reservation in North Dakota and the Rocky Boy Reservation in Montana. Ojibway groups pushed north into the Canadian plains and were later called Cree and Saulteaux Indians. There are even those who say that the Cheyenne, Blackfeet, and Arapaho were part of the Ojibway migration. These groups may have been in such a hurry to reach their chosen ground that they rushed past the Great Lakes region, past the land where food grows on water, and into the plains and mountains of the West.

The free movement of Ojibway tribal groups was slowed considerably after the American colonists gained independence from England and set up their own United States government. The Great Lakes area was then called the North-west Territory but was slowly divided up into states and annexed into the Union. Reservations were drawn up for the Ojibway people that put confines on their hunting and fishing territories and general freedom.

The fur trade gradually diminished with an overwhelming Native dependence on European goods and an already depleted understanding of the traditional ways. The time of the Fifth Fire and "the great struggle" that was predicted to grip the lives of all Native people was already at hand. It was a cultural struggle of the traditional Native way of life pitted against the European way of life. It was a military struggle that had already taken its toll of Native American lives in the eastern United States. Whole tribes of Native people had been wiped out in the name of "progress." The Cherokees in the southeastern United States were moved off of their homelands in 1838 and forced to march to a newly-formed Indian Territory 1200 miles away. A similar fate awaited the great Creek nation in the deep South.

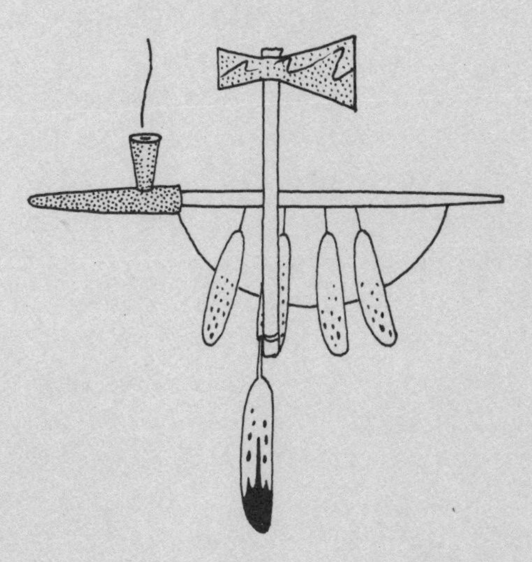

This military struggle spread to the West so as to enforce reservation boundaries and to open up new territories for white settlement. The lure of zhoo-ni-ya-wa-bik' (gold) on the west coast, in the Rocky Mountains, and in the Black Hills of South Dakota served as a stimulus to draw military force and white settlers westward into unprotected Indian lands. The "Indian Wars" on the Great Plains began when Indian nations attempted to defend their homelands. These wars lasted generally from the 1850's to the 1890's and saw countless massacres and dishonorable actions by the U.S. Army and civilians alike.

In 1898, a division of infantry from Fort Snelling, Minnesota was sent by steamboat up the Mississippi River to Leech Lake. They were assigned to put down a revolt of "hostile" Ojibway Indians. The battle that occurred when they arrived at Leech Lake was called "the last of the Indian Wars." The events leading to this battle illustrate the unfairness and trickery that was used in the treatment of Indian people during this era.

Bug-o-nay-gee'-shig (Hole-in-the-Day) was recognized by his people as being the chief of the Ojibway band at Leech Lake. Government agents were trying to get Bug-o-nay-gee'-shig to sell much of the Indian-owned land around the lake. He refused. To get Bug-o-nay-gee'-shig out of the way, the agents accused him of selling whiskey to his people. They arrested him and carried him in chains to Duluth for trial. The judge threw the case out of court due to lack of evidence. Bug-o-nay-gee'-shig was left on his own, without any money, to make his way back to his people at Leech Lake. He made the journey of over 100 miles on foot.

About a week later, Bug-o-nay-gee'-shig was seen at the Indian village of Onigum on Leech Lake. He was there to collect an annuity payment from the Indian agents, a payment promised to all the Leech Lake band in a past treaty with the government. The Indian police in Onigum did not know that Bug-o-nay-gee'-shig had cleared himself in Duluth, and they arrested him. As they were marching him away, a man named Baw-dway'-wi-dun (Sounding Voice) tackled the two policemen, and Bug-o-nay-gee'-shig slipped away. It was news like this that sent rumors flying about an Indian revolt at Leech Lake. It was probably around this time that the troops were dispatched from Fort Snelling.

It was not long after this that fall Midewiwin ceremonies were being held at a place called Sugar Point on Leech Lake. The Ojibway people were giving thanks for a plentiful harvest of wild rice that year. The date was remembered as October 5. A steamboat was spotted on the lake and an alarm was given. Women and children

were sent to Bear Island for safety. The men waited in hiding to see what the occupants of the steamboat intended to do. The steamboat landed at Sugar Point and the troops began to unload and stack their rifles. It is said that in the process of stacking their arms, one of the guns went off. The Indians opened fire on the soldiers. As the battle grew in intensity, the Indians felt they should get their chief, Bug-o-nay-gee'-shig, away from the soldiers. They were able to get two women to take him to Bear Island by canoe. Major Wilson, the officer in charge of the troops, spotted the canoe heading across the water and began firing at it from his position on the steamboat. But each time he fired a wave would come up and hide the canoe and its passengers. Back on shore, an Indian named William Paper or Mahn-see-nay'-e-ganze' (Little Paper) saw the danger his chief was in and carefully took aim at the officer on the steamboat. His shot killed the major. When the troops realized what had happened, they fled to the steamboat and retreated to Walker, Minnesota.

The Battle of Leech Lake cost the lives of 18 soldiers. No Indians were killed. Two Indians were taken prisoner and later tried in Duluth. They were found innocent and released.

This battle was an exception to what typically happened in other battles throughout the western United States during the Indian Wars. Thousands of Indian people were killed to make way for the new America's vision of progress.

Other weapons besides guns were used. In 1879, the U.S. Army barracks at Carlisle, Pennsylvania, were transferred from the War Department to the Interior Department for the "civilizing" of Indian children. In this school and in other boarding schools across the country, Indian children were taken thousands of miles from the support and teachings of their families and taught the ways of the white world. Long hair was cut, gi-shki'-bi-da-gun-nun' (medicine bundles) were burned in huge bonfires, and the speaking of Native language was forbidden.

The Sixth Fire of the Ojibway was kindled at

this time. Grandsons and granddaughters did truly turn against their elders through no choice of their own. The teachings of the elders became weak with few ears to fall on. The elders began to die of a strange sickness. They had lost their reason for living.

This time of attempted assimilation of the Native people of this country was to last for many years. The Bureau of Indian Affairs was formed to be a father figure to the Indian people and to administer programs of leasing out Indian land, selling off Indian land, educating the children, relocating families into the growing American cities, and eventually terminating federal recognition of many Indian tribes.

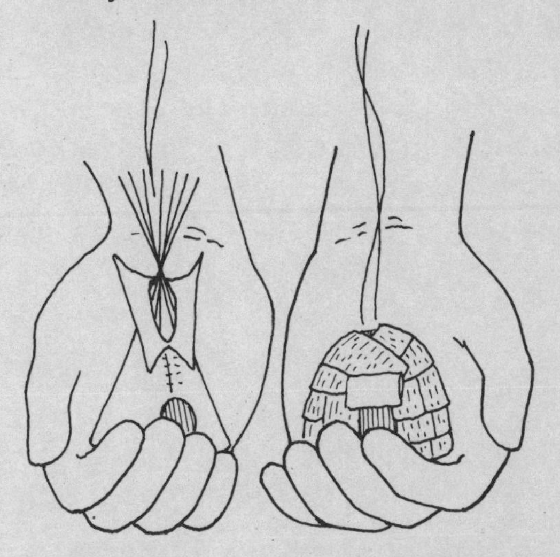

In 1934 Congress passed the Wheeler-Howard Act, better known as the Indian Reorganization Act. This law forced each tribe to abolish its own traditional government and reorganize in a European fashion. Hereafter, the Secretary of the Interior controlled much of the workings of Indian tribal governments.

Back in the days of early European settlement of this country, the Ojibways developed a special name for the Light-skinned Race. They were called Chi-mook'-a-mon-nug' (Long Knives). This name was chosen because of the bayonettes that the whiteman's army used in settling

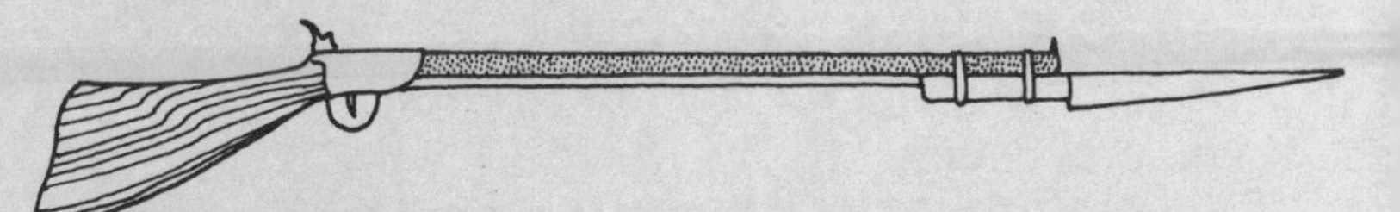

the country. Today, America has replaced the bayonettes with more sophisticated, less visible weapons like school systems that ignore Indian history and culture; textbooks that falsely represent the settlement of this country; and movies and media that misunderstand Indian culture and portray Indian life in a shallow, token way. Still the purpose is the same: to absorb Indian people into the melting pot of American society and to forget the real history of this country and the injustices done to its Native people. The old ways, these teachings, are seen as unnecessary to the modern world. It is becoming more and more evident today that many Americans feel the philosophy advocated by traditional Native people, the respect for all living things, is a roadblock to American progress.

The prophet of the Seventh Fire of the Ojibway spoke of an Osh-ki-bi-ma-di-zeeg'(New People) that would emerge to retrace their steps to find what was left by the trail. There are Indian people today who believe that the New People are with us in the form of our youngest generation. This young generation is searching for their Native language. They are seeking out the few elders who have not forgotten the old ways. They are not finding meaning to their lives in the teachings of American society. They are searching for an understanding of the Earth as Mother of all things. They are finding their way to the Sweat

Lodges, Spirit Ceremonies, Drum Societies, Midewiwin Lodges, Pipe Ceremonies, Longhouse Meetings, Sun Dances, and Kivas that have survived to this day. This younger generation is discovering the common thread that is interwoven among the traditional teachings of all natural people.

There is a minority of Indian people today that seem to be trying to take control over their own lives and the destinies of their children. They are pushing for recognition of the hunting and fishing rights guaranteed to Native people through treaties with the United States. They are seeking payment for and restoration of stolen land. They are trying to re-establish traditional Native religious ceremonies as a day-to-day source of strength and way of living. They are protesting the existence of corrupt, BIA-controlled tribal governments and seeking recognition for traditional forms of Indian government. They are forming their own schools to balance the knowledge of modern survival with the knowledge of Native culture and philosophy.

It is sometimes related by the Ojibway elders of how Chi-bi-shi-kee' (a giant buffalo) has stood at the western doorway looking this way over the lives of the Native people of this land. He is said to be the spirit of the buffalo that guided Waynaboozhoo across the Great Plains on his journey to find his father. This buffalo is a guardian to Indian people everywhere. When life was good for the Native people of this continent and brotherhood, sisterhood, and respect ruled over this land, this buffalo was very powerful. He was the source of much strength for the natural people. His four legs were planted powerfully in the ground like trees. With all his might the buffalo pledged to stand firm in his protection of the natural people.

When the Black Coats came to this country and began to divide the Native people in their devotion to their original instructions, the buffalo lost one of his legs. He sacrificed it so that the Native people could go on living. Still the giant buffalo stood firm at the western doorway even though he only had three legs to support him.

When the armies of the Light-skinned Race came to this country and began to remove Indian people from their homelands, to wipe out entire tribes of the people, and to turn nations against

each other, the giant buffalo in the West sacrificed another leg. He had to stand as best he could on two legs. He was getting weak but he was determined not to fall.

When the grandsons and granddaughters of the Native people began to turn their backs on the teachings of their elders, when the elders lost their reason for living, the buffalo lost yet another leg. Only one leg remained so that he could balance and hold his position in the western doorway. The buffalo knew that if he failed in his task of guardianship, there would be no hope for Indian people to survive. He gathered all his remaining strength and stood fast to his ground.

There he stands today on just one leg, striving as best he can so that Indian people might have a future in this world.

Nokomis and I feel that your presence during these teachings has given strength to the buffalo who stands in the West. He needs our continued support as we seek to find that which was left by the trail. With our help he can regain his legs and give hope to the future of Indian people.

We have compiled all of these teachings from the oral traditions of the Ojibway which have been handed down by the elders to our young people for centuries. There may be those who tell these stories differently, but all interpretations are related to the original teachings that were given to our people.

There are yet more teachings that can teach us how to live in ni-noo'-do-da-di-win.' (harmony) with the Creation. Possibly we can come together in the future to explore more of the traditions of the Ojibway.

Gi '-ga-wa-ba-min' na-gutch'! (See you later!) Mi-gwetch!

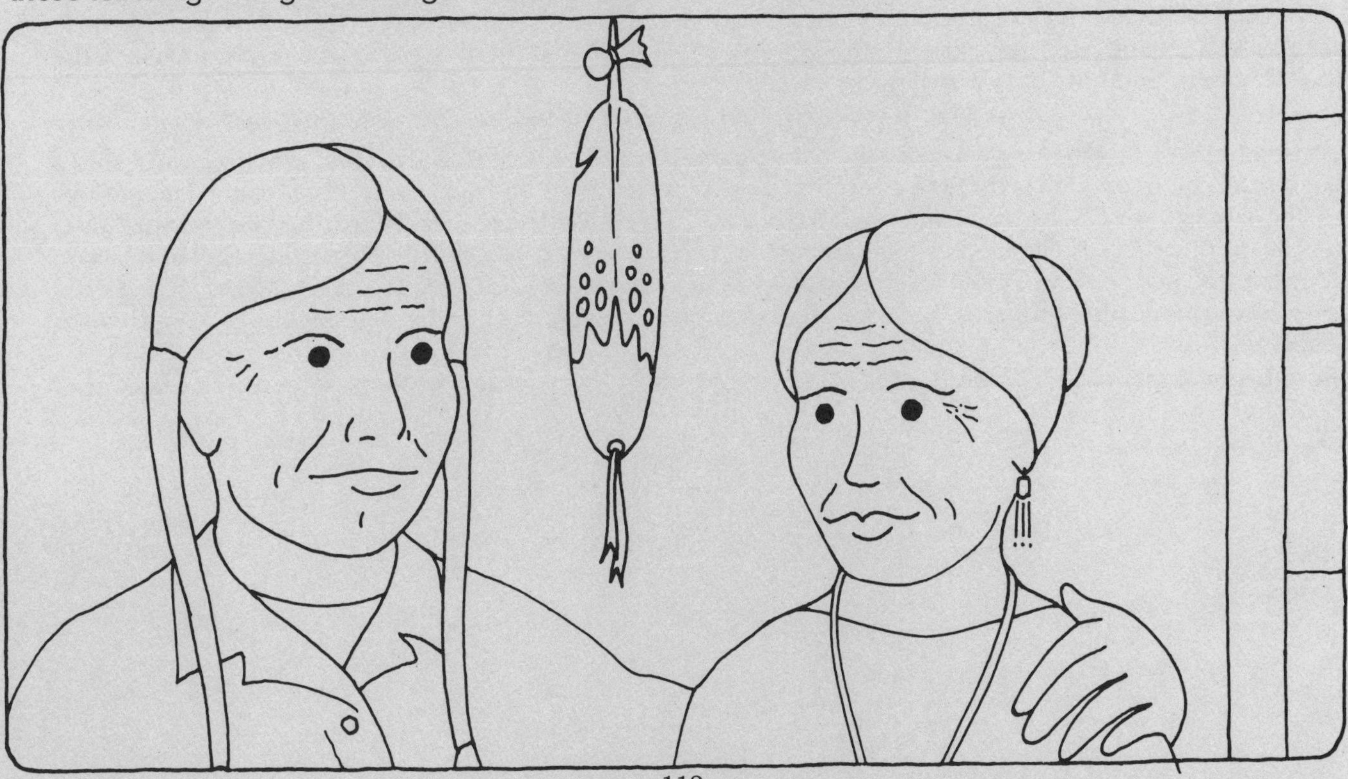

"...Mishomis is Ojibway for grandfather, and this is truly grandfather's book....As a child must be guided to grow in understanding, so does Mishomis take the reader from the simplest beginnings to the complexity of meanings of the Midewiwin and Sweat Lodge Ceremonies. I have not seen anything quite like this before...The Mishomis Book, however, is a spiritual odyssey as well as an historical one, and as such, it is deeply moving. There is so much here that it is impossible to touch on half of it. Although the form is that of a children's book - and I have seldom seen one that I would rather give to a child, Mr. Banai's book is far from being "just" for children. ....The book's usefulness is not limited to those of Native American background. For one thing, it so totally confounds most of the usual Indian stereotypes that I would recommend it highly to anyone who wishes to introduce children of the dominant culture in a more realistic and truthful manner to the lives and culture of the tribal peoples of America. It is hard to imagine that anyone could read this...and not come away from it at least a little more open to the beauty and strangeness of life...."

--Doris Seale Council on Interracial Books for Children

"Here is a unique and fascinating book. It is written by an Indian for Indians. But a non-Indian has the privilege of listening in. It is written by a teacher for young students. But all of us may go to school here and learn important lessons. It is written simply and yet it contains the deepest truths from a great but almost extinguished lore. It is a book about the past and yet it is written for the future. It is therefore a book about the eternal present. It is the voice of the Ojibway people who were and who are to come...We follow the old migrations of the Ojibway people and learn the secrets of their great ceremonies. We who have thought ourselves to be teachers become the taught as we read and meditate. Is it simply coincidence...that we find in these teachings of the Ojibway themes that appear in other ancient cultures also? Or is this indeed a genuine groping with problems that is basic in human nature and as revealing and honourable as any in the story of human thought? The story of the great flood is an illustration.

"...I find in this fascinating and gracious record of Native tradition a discerning inquiry into life's meaning which has been as serious and productive as any other. The parallels show that this tradition has been very close to the highway of human thought....It is a work of grace..."

--Dr. J.W.E. Newberry, Dept. of Native Studies, University of Sudbury, Ontario

"...A wonderful piece of writing which is sure to become a classic. It will be treasured for years to come...(This is a book) written by a traditional Ojibway educator, teacher, writer, and above all, a spiritual man. (The author) comes from a long line of Mide (men and women). His tales come out of the oral tradition of his people (and) gives the book its authenticity, the feeling of past, present and future flowing naturally in a timeless story that has no end...The book brings home to white as well as Indian readers, that for the Native American his Myths are not dead literary museum pieces, but living reality. This is a good book to read by an open fire, a good book to read aloud to your children."

--Richard Erdoes, author of "Lame Deer, Seeker of Visions." "The Sun Dance People," and "The Sound of Flutes."